FROM THE GROUND UP

FROM THE GROUND UP
The Story of a First Garden

by Amy Stewart

St. Martin's Griffin
New York

www.stmartins com

Portions of this book have appeared in a slightly different form in *GreenPrints* and *La Gazette*.

ISBN 0-312-28767-4

First published in the United States by
Algonquin Books of Chapel Hill
A division of Workman Publishing

First St. Martin's Griffin Edition: March 2002

10 9 8 7 6 5 4 3 2 1

To my parents, Vic and Dee Stewart

Contents

A Growing Season

Planting the Seed

GARDENS DON'T HAPPEN BY THEMSELVES. They don't come about by accident. A few seeds blow into a backyard, or sunflowers start to grow along the highway, or a row of strawberries flourishes up and down the train tracks—but these migrations of plants, these volunteers, are not gardens. A garden is a human creation. It has to be thought of first. It has to be wished into being, planned for, like a wanted child.

At least, that's how my garden began. I am a daughter of the suburbs, where yards are for grass and grass alone, where flowers come from the supermarket in cellophane wrappers and spinach is sold in frozen blocks. I remember one garden from my childhood, a garden I saw one day when my parents took me house-hunting with them. I was about seven, my brother was five, and we were all tired of living in apartments. We want our own bedrooms, my brother and I would chant from the backseat, and we want a yard. We drove from one house to another, and each one looked just like the next—brick tract homes surrounded by patches of just-mowed St. Augustine grass. Only one house stands out in my mind, a flat ranch house like all the others, but the backyard had been transformed into a leafy, overgrown vegetable garden. I had never seen anything like it. Strawberries rambled along the ground, down low where I could see them. The old man who lived in the house was bent down among them, hiding out from the realtor, picking berries. When he saw me, he nudged me toward the strawberries, told me not to worry about the dirt, just eat. I ate them in small nibbles, letting their wild sweet flavor run around my mouth, and put the chewed-off stems carefully into my pocket.

He showed me how to eat the peas climbing the fence. Grasp one end of the pod and break it, hard but not too hard, so a string remains attached and works like a zipper to open the pod. Pick the peas out, one at a time. I traced the inside of the pod with my tongue and the peas popped away from the seam into my mouth. Their taste summoned up everything I loved about summer—grass and crickets and swimming pools, and the good warm sun itself. I kept the pea pods, stuffing them into my pocket along with the wet tails of the strawberries. I pulled them out that night, back at home, where they seemed messy and irrelevant among the toys and books that crowded my room.

I didn't think about gardening again until graduate school, when I noticed the front yards in my Austin neighborhood as I walked by on my way to class. I waved shyly at my neighbors, mostly graduate students or young professors, who stood outdoors among their flowers, watering their gardens before the sun started to beat down. What were they doing? Didn't they have to go to class? Shouldn't they be studying? The thought of allowing that kind of diversion from my own work seemed careless, irresponsible. But as I watched them tend their gardens in the evenings, on the weekends, or during an occasional stolen afternoon when I knew they must be playing hooky from school, I started to envy them. They were outdoors with their shovels and their boots, turning the earth, calling to each other from across the fence. After graduation, faced with the prospect of spending a lifetime working in an office under artificial lights, I yearned for what they had—a way to get outdoors and get my hands dirty, to create something, to help something grow. I met my husband, Scott, in graduate school, and as classes wound down for the last time, we talked about moving to California together. California, in my mind, was green and tropical all year long. Anything would grow in California. "I want a garden when we get to the coast," I told Scott, "a house with a yard where I can plant something."

If I had asked my neighbors at the time, they might have been able to tell me that gardening is about more than putting plants in the ground. When you set out to work on a garden, something surprising happens. The garden goes to work on you, too. In the process of bringing a patch of earth to life, your life is transformed.

I would find out about that soon enough, though, and so would Scott. When we moved to California, it didn't take us long to find a place where I could plant my first garden.

Breaking Ground

First Garden

*Making a garden is not a gentle hobby for the elderly, to be
picked up and laid down like a game of solitaire. It is a grand
passion. It seizes a person whole, and once it has done so he will
have to accept that his life is going to be radically changed.*

—MAY SARTON, Plant Dreaming Deep, 1968

The garden didn't look like much at first:
bare dirt, a couple of fruit trees, and a few
shrubs. The previous tenants had not bothered much
with gardening, and that was fine with me. I didn't want
to take up the work that someone else had left unfinished.
I wanted full credit for whatever this garden turned out
to be.

The house was an old California bungalow, light brown
with dark brown trim, a little drab compared to the brilliant whitewash and the pastel beach colors of the other

houses in the neighborhood. There were three windows in the front: our bedroom window on the left, then the windows that wrap around what used to be the porch and later became an entryway, and on the right, an enormous living room window that filled the house with light, and faced west to frame hazy, salmon-colored sunsets in the summer. Six wooden steps led from the front door to the patio, where you could sit in the old metal glider and look across the street to the ocean.

There was no front yard, just a short strip of land under the windows, barely enough room to bother planting anything at all. All the houses on our street sat on a hill that sloped down to the river, and they were all built about five feet above the sidewalk. If you walked past our house, the garden was at eye level. Everyone planted something along their retaining walls to make the neighborhood look interesting from the street. The people at the end of our block planted a formal boxwood hedge. Our next door neighbors planted pink ivy geraniums. But we were stuck with the landlord's choice, African daisy, an uninspiring ground cover with purple and white daisylike flowers. Boring, I thought when we moved in, freeway plants. African daisies grew on the highway median strips in Santa Cruz. They seemed far too commonplace for the kind of garden I had in mind.

The side yard was just an expanse of bare dirt, a few scraggly rosebushes, and a pink jasmine vine. This would become the perennial flower border, the place where only the toughest, woodiest shrubs would survive the onslaught of ocean wind every spring. I didn't know that at the time. "We're planting tulips," I said firmly to Scott. I was fearless then. I was ready to try anything.

The backyard had not been touched in years, but some tenant, maybe twenty or thirty years earlier, had given some thought to what a garden as small as this one should have: wisteria, the first heady fragrance of the spring; an orange tree and a lemon tree, practically standard issue in California gardens; fuchsia, to entice the hummingbirds, and because—well, because if you *can* grow a fuchsia, you *should*. They grow all over Santa Cruz; they flourish in this climate. I have seen tourists walk by them and touch the flowers, cautiously, as if they were touching wet paint. "Is it real?" they ask. One time I heard someone answer, "Is *anything* real around here?"

I NEVER THOUGHT I'd live in a beach town like Santa Cruz. If you ever wondered whether people who live at the seashore take it for granted after a while, let me tell you: We don't. At least, I never have. To wake up to the sound of harbor seals barking under the municipal wharf,

to breathe the fishy salt air every morning—there is nothing better. The Pacific is never the same from one day to the next. Sometimes it is wild and dramatic, even inside the bay where I live. The waves rear up, taller than me, and pound against the sand, sending sea foam flying in every direction. Other days, the sea is flat and calm and almost warm enough for swimming, a study in blues: the flat glass of the ocean, the bright blue of the sky, the faded blue paint of the lifeguard stands.

I walked on the beach once with my aunt D'Anna, who was visiting me from Texas. We were talking about our jobs; we each had our own kind of job stress at the time. "But you see," I explained, "I come here at the end of the day. No matter how bad it is, I always know that there is *this* waiting for me. Sort of makes everything else seem unimportant." Some nights I see a flock of pelicans diving for anchovies, and sometimes a low tide lays sand dollars and beach glass at my feet. I come home with my pockets full of treasures, and they litter the front porch: the seashells, the dried-out seaweed, the beach glass in a jar. There is always sand in the entryway—you can't keep it out. It dusts the front steps and trails inside like bread crumbs.

We live in the very center of the tourist attractions, just one block from the ocean, right across the street from the

Santa Cruz Beach Boardwalk, an old-fashioned seaside amusement park. Our view of the ocean is framed by the wooden grid of the roller coaster. Because of this, our house shows up on postcards all the time. How many people can say that? I began collecting postcards as soon as we moved in. I carried them around and showed them to anyone who would pay attention. "Look!" I would say, pointing with the tip of a pen. "See there, just behind the roller coaster? Up on the hill? That's our house! We *live* there! We can hear the people screaming on the roller coaster from our living room!" Usually our house appears on these postcards as a little brown blob, but once I found a calendar that showed it clearly in the background, set back from the beach, behind the Boardwalk: a light brown California bungalow, perched high above the street, the sunlight glinting off the three big windows across the front of the house. You can almost see the red geraniums on the front porch. Almost.

SCOTT AND I FOUND THIS HOUSE TOGETHER, after two years of living apart in California. We had arrived at the worst possible time, when jobs were scarce and state employees were paid with vouchers instead of cash. We could not find jobs in the same town, so he moved to Eureka, a coastal town just south of the Oregon border, and I settled in Santa Cruz. It was hard, living apart like that; even though we hadn't yet married, we'd grown accustomed to living together in graduate school, and we felt each other's absence intensely. We had to drive seven hours to see each other, which limited us to long weekends together every month or two. After one of those weekends, we couldn't face the prospect of returning alone to our empty apartments. The separation had gone on too long. Making a life together had become more important than pursuing our separate careers. Scott quit his job and came to join me in Santa Cruz, and I got ready to leave my cramped little place in the mountains in favor of this house, which was big enough for the two of us and, at last, gave me a place where I could plant something. When Scott showed up in Santa Cruz, he brought an oregano plant that he'd dug up from his yard in Eureka for me to plant in my garden.

I should say here and now that it was my garden from the beginning. Good thing, too, because it was scarcely big enough for one of us, much less both of us. I have heard about marriages in which the wife takes the vegetable garden, the husband the flower garden. Or one farms the south pasture while the other tends the orchard. Nothing like that would have worked in our tiny Santa Cruz garden, which seemed laughably small compared to the wide swaths of grass that surround every house back in Texas. Still, it was a good place to start. It was just right for a first garden.

I SPENT A LOT OF TIME walking around the garden after we moved in, thinking about what I wanted it to look like. I couldn't picture it exactly—trying to picture your future garden is a little like trying to picture the person you'll marry—the image was blurred and constantly changing. Should there be a patio? What could I grow under the citrus trees? Where would I plant the vegetable garden—or should I just tuck the vegetables in among the flowers and let them go wild?

At least I knew what I didn't want: a garden like the ones I remembered from the suburban Texas tract house that we finally settled on after that long day of house-hunting. Most of the plants I hate today grew at that house. Nandina, a dull, unimaginative shrub with leaves the color of cockroaches and stingy little berries that—when I was foolish enough to put one in my mouth—tasted like pennies. Century plants, whose fleshy gray arms grabbed me as I walked by, scraping my calves with thorns as long as fingernails. And that boring old lawn, that expanse of St. Augustine grass, where my grandfather and uncles would gather to pluck weeds during family barbecues, squatting down and pulling crabgrass in silence while they waited for the football game to come on. I wish I could say that I had some sweet memory of a childhood garden I wanted to re-create. But the fact is, there wasn't a single plant around our house that I could love, nothing at all to inspire me as I thought about planting my first garden in Santa Cruz.

I remembered the gardens in Austin, the sweet ambitious jumbles of flowers and vegetables. Those gardens struck a chord in me. They were wild and untamed, but entirely welcoming at the same time. You could have *fun* in gardens like those. They were full of surprises: the poppies that went to seed in the lettuce bed, the alyssum that sprang from cracks in the sidewalk, the flowering vine that snaked its way up an oak tree and bloomed there all summer. These gardens were not afraid to be different from the rest. They spilled over their borders, they clashed with the neighbors, they ran amuck.

This was the kind of garden I wanted: a lively and boisterous place, part miniature farm, part playground, part zoo. A place where I could grow purple tomatoes and plant rainbow stripes of lettuce and let the sparrows pick seeds out of the sunflowers. A place that would abound with bugs and butterflies and the faint, rustling sound of things growing. I had no idea how I'd go about it, but I couldn't wait to get my hands into the dirt and get started.

I didn't know what I was getting myself into, during those first few weeks, when I had nothing but bare ground and a head full of garden fantasies. How could I have known? Who, before they begin to garden, could predict that they would ever lie awake at night worrying over a tray of seedlings, become obsessed with rotting leaves, order worms and insect larvae through the mail? Who could guess that dirt and manure and blood meal would become topics of conversation around the dinner table, or that the human dramas of love and birth and death would play themselves out between the ladybugs and the aphids, among the unfurling leaves of an artichoke?

When I looked out over the expanse of dirt, I could hardly believe that it was mine to plant. Soon, I would be outside with seeds and a shovel, making a garden.

Making a Sun Map

If I had it to do over again, I would have waited a little while before I planted my first garden. I would have watched the weather patterns, noticing which parts of the yard got hit hardest by rains and salty sea winds, and I would have made a sun map of the backyard to help me figure out what to plant where. The entire garden measured no more than twelve hundred square feet, including the twenty-five- by forty-foot rectangle in the back, the eight-foot-wide side yard, and the skinny strip of land along the front. There were only a few spots anywhere that were clear of the shadows of the house, the fence, or the neighbors' trees.

To make a sun map, go outside early in the morning with a ball of twine and some stakes or, if you want to feed the garden while you map it, use a highly visible powder like bonemeal or diatomaceous earth. Mark the boundaries of the shade cast by the house, the fence, and the trees. Repeat the process at noon and again in the late afternoon. At the end of the day, you'll have a map of the garden that shows you the sunniest and the shadiest areas for planting. If I had done this in the beginning, I would have known to divide my vegetable garden into two medium-sized rectangles, one on either side of the citrus trees, with a border around each for shade-tolerant vegetables like lettuce and parsley. Instead, I couldn't wait to get started, so I dug myself one large, awkward rectangle in the corner, half in the shade of the trees, and made a patio in the only other sunny spot. This is a decision that I often regretted but never got around to changing.

Weeds

The man who worries morning and night about the dandelions in the lawn will find great relief in loving the dandelions.

—L. H. BAILEY, Manual of Gardening, 1910

My father is a guitarist. I grew up watching him practice, perched on a bar stool in the kitchen or on the edge of the couch in the living room, in front of the television, playing scales or riffs or a song he had to learn for a gig. I didn't have a very strong ear for music, so I didn't really know what my father was doing when he practiced. I heard notes and melodies that grew so familiar to me, after having heard them in the background for weeks at a time, that after a while I couldn't even remember where I'd heard them in the first place.

When I tried to learn to play the guitar myself, I finally realized what he'd been doing every day. He'd been picking up his guitar at the appointed time, with a metronome and a sheet of music in front of him, and allowing himself to fail. Not just once, but over and over, and every day. When I watch him practice now, I still can't hear the mistakes, but I can see them in his face: His concentration breaks, his eyes open, and he mutters *no, no . . . not that* and begins again, without hesitating, without taking his hands off the guitar. Because this is the only way you learn a piece of music, by making mistakes. By playing it wrong, over and over again, until finally, someday, you play it right.

It didn't occur to me that the same might be true of gardening, that gardening, like music, could demand practice, patience, a willingness to make mistakes. Planting a garden seemed so simple, so straightforward, as I thought about it while Scott and I unpacked and got settled into our new house. I envisioned flower beds, climbing vines, rows of corn and peas. How hard could it be? I had land of my own, a shovel in the garage, a nursery down the street ready to supply the plants. All the necessary ingredients were there. What could possibly go wrong?

I could just picture us on the weekends: Scott, who spent his Saturdays building a business as a rare book dealer, would sit at the computer cataloging books from his collection. I would work outside in the garden, hauling shovels and rakes around with me, bringing in armloads of flowers and vegetables that I'd grown. I would pass by our living room window from time to time and tap the glass to get Scott's attention. He would look up, smile, and we would wave at each other and return to our work. It wasn't hard to imagine. In fact, it seemed like we'd already been living that way our whole lives. I felt like I'd always been a gardener. And, as we settled into bed on the Friday night after we moved in, I fell asleep knowing that the unpacking was finished and a free Saturday stretched out in front of me. I was ready to get out into the garden, and it seemed like I knew all I needed to know to get started.

THAT FIRST SATURDAY MORNING ARRIVED, full of bustle and noise. "What *is* that?" Scott groaned, pulling the covers over his head.

I listened for a minute. "I think it's the roller coaster."

He lifted his head high enough off the pillow to see the alarm clock. "It's eight o'clock. What's going on out there?"

"Maybe they're testing the ride." I lay in bed and listened to the car ratchet up the tracks and speed down the other side. I could tell there were no people on the ride; it made a hollow rattling sound as it ran through its paces, over and over, without stopping at the end of the ride to pick up passengers as it normally would. I was only just beginning to realize that living this close to an amusement park was a little like living at the circus. There was always something going on. Except in the dead of winter, my days would be driven by the sounds and smells drifting over from the Boardwalk: the creaky metal gates opening early in the morning to let in the employees, the smell of corn dogs and cotton candy around lunchtime, and, late in the evening, long after dark, the lights of the roller coaster turning off suddenly as if to signal to the entire neighborhood that the party was over and it was time to go to bed.

In spite of the commotion, I loved waking up in our new house. There was always some reminder that we lived at the ocean, some sound drifting into our bedroom. Occasionally, if there was no noise from the Boardwalk to block it out, I would wake to the sound of waves crashing against the sand. Once, we left the window open all night and when the breeze shifted after sunrise, the smell of the salt air alone was enough to wake me.

There was a break in the rain that Saturday morning, a good omen for my first day in the garden. The rainy season here begins in late October and ends in April. During the rest of the year, it might not rain once. I couldn't get used to that when we first moved to California. I grew up with dark, dramatic Texas thunderstorms, the kind that can roll in on an afternoon and send everyone running for cover. Every outdoor event in Texas has a rain plan, some indoor alternative in case of a storm. Nobody makes rain plans in California, I realized. If it's summer, it will be clear, and if it's winter, it will rain.

I hadn't really thought about what this meant for gardeners, but I figured it out as soon as I stepped outside that February morning. It had been raining almost every day since we moved in—enough to soak the ground and get everything growing. A light mist hung around the garden, draping itself across the dormant wisteria vine, the citrus trees, and the camellia just beginning to bud. I was so captivated by the sight of my garden that it took me a minute to look down at my feet, to the ground I was hoping to begin planting in that morning. When I did, I was startled by what I saw. I had *weeds!* Not just a few weeds, but a nearly uninterrupted carpet of them, where just last week there had been nothing but bare dirt. Where did they come from? What *were* they? I bent down to look closer. Each stem held three heart-shaped leaves, almost like a clover leaf. Well, I thought, reassured, clover isn't such a bad thing to have in the backyard. I wasn't sure if clover could even be considered a weed. Didn't farmers grow clover in their fields? Didn't bees make honey out of it?

It took a trip to the nursery to look through the

gardening books before I figured out what I had: yellow oxalis. "A very aggressive weed," according to the *Sunset Western Garden Book,* which I was guilt-tripped into buying after being scoffed at by the man who worked at the nursery. "Did you look it up in the *Garden Book?*" he asked, when I came in to describe my weed. I looked around, confused, at all the garden books on the shelf.

"Which one?" I asked. He made an impatient little sucking sound with his teeth.

"*The* garden book," he said, handing me a copy of Sunset's six-hundred-page reference book. "I can see you haven't been gardening long."

No, just about a half an hour, I wanted to say, but then he was gone. I turned back to my new reference book. "Gardeners in central and southern California rate it especially troublesome," the book said about my weed. "Control is difficult."

By the time I got back home, Scott was awake and standing out on the front porch. "Where did you go?" he asked, blinking in the daylight.

"I've been to the nursery trying to figure out what to do about *this,*" I said grimly, gesturing toward the weeds that were sprouting everywhere, even in the cracks on the porch.

Scott didn't have his glasses on. He bent over the ground

and scrutinized the weeds from a distance of a couple of inches. "It looks like clover," he said.

I rolled my eyes. "It's not *clover,* silly," I said impatiently. "It's oxalis."

"Oxalis," he repeated. "What do you know about it?"

"It's especially troublesome."

Troublesome was right. I was hoping to make some half-start toward a little garden on my first day out, something that I could stand over proudly at the end of the day, beaming and dusting off my hands. Instead, I had to pull *weeds*. I felt like I'd been told to go clean my room.

I had a tedious task ahead of me. Oxalis forms a deep taproot that looks like a thick, pasty-white worm when it's pulled up and tossed onto the pavement. If you want to get rid of a weed, you might think that pulling it up by the root is the only way to get it out of the garden. After all, any bits of root left in the soil could regrow and sprout again before the season's over. But when I sat down cross-legged among the oxalis that morning and tried pulling it out of the ground, I realized that I was actually helping it reproduce. By yanking it out of the dirt, I was stripping off all the tiny bulbs that grew along the root and contained within them the beginnings of next year's oxalis crop. It was probably the best thing anyone could do to get them off to a good start for the spring. Even though I knew I was doing no good, I couldn't bring myself to stop pulling them up. I just had to get something accomplished. I had to have something to show for my time. I yanked them up by the handful, tossing them into a pile on the pavement. When I looked up, all I saw around me was more oxalis. So this is gardening, I thought, discouraged. It's not exactly what I had in mind.

By the end of the day, I managed to clear less than half the bed that runs along the side of the house, and even then I didn't get every single oxalis plant. Scraggly clumps of them lurked around the corners of the bed, and a few roots clung stubbornly to the soil, with nothing but a ripped-off stem remaining above ground.

I couldn't see myself pulling weeds every weekend for the next few months. Somewhere, deep down, I knew that the wise thing to do would be to spend the last few weeks of winter preparing the garden and to hold off on planting anything until the spring, when the ground was ready, when I was ready. But I couldn't wait that long. I just wanted a quick and easy way of getting rid of the weeds so I could get on to the real business of gardening: Planting flowers. Making things grow.

I thought about digging the oxalis bulbs out of the soil one at a time. Scott tried it a few days later and ended up spending an entire afternoon sifting through about two square feet of dirt, meticulously picking out of the ground every pea-shaped, dirt-colored oxalis bulb he could find and putting it in a little pile next to him on the pavement. The dirt stayed fresh and crumbly and free of weeds for a few days, and then the oxalis grew back as if nothing had happened.

Perhaps the secret was to get them while they were young, before they had a chance to reproduce. I tried this for a while, but I just didn't have the patience for it. Looking out over the thousands of seedlings that had already sprouted, I knew I didn't stand a chance of keeping up with them, and I just got too discouraged. If I had a very small plot of land—just a few feet, maybe—and I didn't have a job or anything else that took up much of my time, I could patrol my yard every day, looking for oxalis. I could remove each tiny sprout, maybe with a pair of tweezers, and drop it into the trash. I would have to do this every day for about six months, even in the rain, even in the cold. Then I would probably have to repeat the whole procedure next year, and the year after. Oxalis bulbs can live for years in the soil, I learned after I did a little more research. They don't give up easily.

It embarrassed me, this messy, weedy yard. I felt like a bad housekeeper, like I'd left my dirty dishes in the sink.

But what could I do, if I wasn't going to spend all day every day picking them out of the ground? Learn to live with them? Plant around them? Hope to outnumber them, to crowd them out with whatever I decided to plant?

At least I could be comforted by the fact that oxalis grew everywhere. I wasn't the only one. I started noticing it in my neighbors' yards, in the spaces between the sidewalk downtown, and even growing in large masses along the highway up the coast. In February it started producing an iridescent yellow, trumpet-shaped blossom. "It's kind of pretty," Scott said, when he saw me looking sadly out the kitchen window at my patch of flowering weeds. One time, a little boy even stopped in front of my house and starting picking them out of the cracks in the bottom steps. His parents were following slowly behind him, lost in conversation, paying him no attention. He had six or seven of them in his hand before he noticed me sitting at the top of the stairs, watching him. I was touched that somebody could see the beauty in a weed I'd already learned to hate. I remembered the wonder I'd felt when, as a child, I'd found a dandelion gone to seed, ready for me to make a wish and blow it away. I didn't know then that a dandelion was a weed.

That's the great thing about kids—they don't discriminate. Maybe I could learn something from this. Maybe oxalis wasn't so bad. I bet other people hadn't even noticed all the weeds in my yard. Maybe, like this little boy, all they saw were bright yellow flowers spreading a little cheer on a gray February day.

When the boy saw me looking at him, he dropped the oxalis, startled that he'd been caught. I laughed. "Go ahead," I told him, as his parents caught up with him. "Pick all the flowers you want."

"Nice try," his father said, grinning at me. Then, looking at his son, he said, "Josh, you don't want those any more than she does. Those aren't flowers. They're *weeds*."

Cultivating Weeds

I paid no attention to this gardening tip in my first year, so I hardly expect any other new gardeners to take it seriously. Who, once they have been consumed with gardening fever, once the sweet pea seedlings have started to crowd the back porch, could bear to delay planting for even a couple of weeks while they cultivated a bed of weeds? But eventually I tried this little trick, and it has served me well over the years.

Once you clear a bed for planting, put down a thick layer of compost or manure and water the bed as if you'd just planted a row of seeds. Keep the bed moist for a week or two until sprouts appear. These represent the next generation of weeds, the ones that would have been popping up next to your flowers or your vegetables had you gone ahead and planted. Drag a rake across the bed, pulling up seedlings as you go, and water again. After a few more days, the next wave of seedlings will come up, sparser than the first. Repeat the process with the rake and the water for another week or two, until most of the weed seeds and root systems have exhausted themselves. This requires a great deal of patience, but you will be rewarded: Your flowers will have room to grow with almost no competition from the weeds.

Neighbors

Visiting neighboring gardens is another important part
of a head gardener's duty. This should be done with a view
not only to order and neatness, but also to good culture,
intelligence, as to the state of gardening, &c.

—JANE LOUDON,
Loudon's Encyclopadia of Gardening, 1830

I realized early on that commenting on your
neighbor's garden was an essential part of life
here. We crowd up against each other in this old neighborhood, making it impossible not to look over the
fence and raise an eyebrow. There were roses on one
side of me, potted geraniums on the other, and across
the street, a large and well-tended rhubarb patch. I
began to know people by the plants that grew in their
yards: There was the Trumpet Vine Lady up the street,
the Cherry Blossom Guy a couple blocks over, and the

Aloe Couple who just moved in down by the beach and inherited a front yard that was dominated by an aloe plant the size of a small car.

Each street is a hodgepodge of Santa Cruz history. The beach cottages all cluster together near the harbor, where they once provided a weekend home for wealthy Bay Area tourists who were brave enough to travel the narrow, treacherous highway down the coast. The gracious old Victorians perch on the bluff just up the hill from us, high above town, the place where some of Santa Cruz's oldest families showed off the money they'd made from fishing in Monterey Bay. And then there is block after block of houses like ours: Craftsman-style bungalows from the twenties and thirties used as vacation homes for people like the doctor in San Francisco who took ours from a patient as payment and used it as a fishing place for twenty years.

Apart from driving through the narrow streets to go to work or the grocery store, I hadn't seen much of my neighborhood so far, so one day I decided to walk around and check it out. It was a bright day on the cusp between winter and spring, one of the few sunny days we'd had so far that year, but already, young flowers were blooming up and down my street. Since we moved in during the winter, among the clouds and the rain, I hadn't really noticed how vibrant Santa Cruz could be on a sunny day. Most of the houses here were painted bright beach colors: lemon yellow, mint green, carnation pink, and blues as varied as the colors of the ocean and the sky.

The gardens had a laid-back attitude, very appropriate for a beach town. Forget about manicured lawns, they seemed to say as I walked past them. Avoid anything that looks too much like "landscaping". Life is short—plant *everything*. In just two blocks, I saw tomatoes growing in a rose garden, generous stretches of poppy and yarrow where anyone else would plant grass, and artichokes lining someone's back fence, along an alley, where the silvery thistle leaves emerged between the nasturtiums. Many of the front yards were shoulder-to-shoulder flowers and blooming shrubs. Some people grew their vegetables in the front in raised beds, to take full advantage of the sun. The old Victorians had ancient, overgrown gardens shaded by enormous redwoods that never got cleared when the houses were first built. The gardens were mostly screened from view by tall hedges and tangles of climbing roses. As if in defiance of all that wilderness, a few houses had only geometric rock gardens, tidy designs laid out in minimalist red and white rock.

Of all the plants I saw, though, the one I noticed most often was oxalis. Everyone had it. I had decided to learn to live with mine, which felt like progress. I was taking a relaxed attitude, less like a worried parent and more like one of those beloved aunts who will let you eat ice cream for breakfast. Let the weeds come, I thought. There are more important things to do. I'll tidy up later.

Not everyone took this approach, though. Some people had nearly immaculate yards, with only a few tiny oxalis sprouts. They seemed to be trying the "hand-pick every new plant before it can reproduce" technique, the one that requires that you take significant time off from your job just to keep ahead of it. I envied those people. I wanted to be one of them, but I knew that I never would be. I identified a little more with the people who ripped the plant up, but left the root and a bit of the stem in the ground. They just wanted to get something done. They wanted to see some progress, even if they knew that all the roots they left in the ground would sprout new weeds sooner or later.

I got advice as I walked. A few blocks away from my house, there was an ugly green duplex, completely out of place between the stately Victorians on either side. There was one small patch of yard in front, in an area about eight feet by ten. It was so completely packed with flowers that at first I didn't notice the woman who was crouched down planting seeds behind a stand of tall foxglove. She looked wildly happy, there in her garden, in an old blue housecoat and a pair of hiking boots. I understood why she looked so joyous—her garden was brimming over, there was not an empty spot anywhere. Everything was in bloom, from the tiny primroses that bordered the sidewalk, to the pink and white cosmos, to the climbing roses around her front door. And not a single oxalis in sight. When I asked her about it, she told me that she used black plastic landscaping fabric to keep the weeds down. And lots of compost, she added, waving an empty plastic bag of it around.

Suddenly, I couldn't wait to get back to my own garden and start planting. I hadn't realized a garden could be this far along so early in the year. I was beginning to feel behind already. I made mental notes as I walked, adding new gardening terms to my vocabulary: *compost, landscape fabric*.

I was within a few blocks of my house when I almost tripped over a pile of wrinkled brown bulbs sitting on the sidewalk, still covered in dirt, and a hand-lettered cardboard sign that read, "Crocosmia. Flaming Orange Flowers. Take Some Home." In the yard, there was a newly dug bed planted with larkspur where the crocosmia must have been. The larkspur were blue and wispy, and I could see why the owner had dug the bulbs up: "flaming orange" would not have gotten along with larkspur at all. I looked around to see if the person who'd left them on the sidewalk was still outside, but there was no one around. I picked up a few of them and turned them over in my hand. They were round, flattened things wrapped in a stringy husk that looked more like a piece of burlap than anything that would grow in the ground. It was hard to imagine any flower emerging from those squat little bulbs, much less one that was too wild to share a flower bed with the civilized, pastel larkspur.

I didn't have such conflicts to worry about in my own garden, at least not yet. I could start out with crocosmia and take it from there. Everything else I planted would just have to learn to get along with them. I took a few of them, left the rest for someone else to find, and walked home, savoring the rustle of the papery bulbs in my jacket pocket. I felt welcome. It was better than a casserole, this housewarming gift from the neighbors.

MY NEXT-DOOR NEIGHBOR CHARLIE was outside pulling weeds when I got back. He and his wife, Beverly, lived in the white stucco house on our right. A row of pink ivy geraniums bloomed in front, and behind it, a bank of fragrant star jasmine. His garden looked orderly, cared for. It looked like someone was tending it, taking it seriously, and in fact, someone was. Charlie glanced over the fence at my pile of brown bulbs. "What are you planting?"

I tried to sound confident as I pronounced it: "Crocosmia." Then, in case there were several varieties, I added, "Flaming orange flowers."

He nodded. "Yes, I know. You mean these?" and he pointed to a clump of young, spiky leaves, just pushing their way out of the ground. Half of them stood in his yard and the other half in mine.

"That's crocosmia?" I couldn't believe it.

"Yep. It grows along the alley, too. If you want some more, you can go out there and dig some up."

I had already begun to rip out the African daisy to make room for them. I sat down among the mess I was making in my front yard, feeling a little foolish. I should have known better. Who would leave anything but the most common plant out on the sidewalk, free for the taking? Everybody had crocosmia, apparently, which was why you couldn't even give it away, except to newcomers like me.

One advantage of living in a neighborhood where everybody talked to everybody else was that it didn't take me long to continue the cycle of giving away unwanted plants. The Trumpet Vine Lady came by the next day and asked if she could have some of the African daisies I'd ripped out to make room for the crocosmia. I felt a little silly, digging around in my pile of wilted, ripped-out plants to find something to give her, but it made its own kind of crazy sense, trying to get rid of my unwanted plants so I could make room for somebody else's unwanted plants. Sort of like holding a garage sale to make room for all the stuff you bought at other people's garage sales. She gathered up the African daisies and headed back to her house. I sat down on the porch steps and watched her go. The ripped-out plants in her hands looked like two giant, grotesque flower bouquets, the kind of thing Frankenstein's monster might pick out for his bride, with flowers sticking out in every direction, scraggly brown roots hanging down almost to her knees, and clods of dirt falling to the ground.

After she rounded the bend in the road and disappeared from sight, I jumped down from the steps and stood in the street to take in the full effect of the work I'd done so far. The oxalis was cleared away, at least for the moment, and where the African daisies had been, a neat square of earth was now planted with bulbs and raked smooth. Any day now, the crocosmia would start to push tiny green sprouts through the dirt, and the hummingbirds would hover nearby, waiting for the flaming orange flowers to bloom.

The Neighborly Art of Propagation

Sharing plants is one of the best parts of living in a neighborhood full of gardeners. It is a way of passing on not just plants, but advice, too. "I've got extra artichokes," a woman down the street once said, handing me two sturdy young plants. "Take them, you'll want them in your flower arrangements come fall." It wasn't until I left an artichoke on the stalk one October and watched it open into a bright blue thistle that I knew what she meant. People give plants away as insurance, too: If you've passed out a few iris rhizomes every fall, you can be sure that some neighbor will have a few to give back to you should yours get nibbled by gophers. The problem was, I was not always sure what to do with the vines, twigs, and clumps of roots once they were handed over the fence to me.

As it turns out, there is an entire science devoted to taking cuttings and making them grow. To do it properly, you need equipment, powders and potions, and plenty of patience. Here's a basic list of ingredients, along with some instructions, to get you started:

> Rooting compound, powder or liquid (available at most
>   nurseries)
> Fungicide
> Slow-release fertilizer
> Scalpel or garden knife
> Alcohol and candle for sterilizing the knife
> Seed-starting tray
> Growing medium, such as a mixture of half peat moss
>   and half small bark
> Mist sprayer

Fill a seed-starting tray with growing medium; mist thoroughly.

Sterilize your knife by dipping it in alcohol and passing it quickly through a candle flame.

Take a cutting just above the leaf node, and remove all side shoots and lower leaves with your knife. Then make a "wound" near the base of the stem by trimming off a sliver of bark, which will expose the part of the plant in which cell division takes place.

Dip the base of the cutting, including the wound, into the rooting compound, and insert it into a seed-starting tray filled with growing medium. Spray thoroughly with fungicide. Repeat the applications of fungicide every two weeks, keep the growing medium evenly moist, and feed regularly with a slow-release fertilizer.

Rootings can take several weeks to several months.

There is another method, one that I've used when I was short on time and patience: I thank the neighbor for the cutting, stick it in the ground, water, and wait. Some of the cuttings grow. Some of them don't. I just hope the neighbors never ask to come over and see how their cuttings are doing in my garden. So far, I've been lucky; they haven't asked.

Cats

A garden without cats, it will be generally agreed, can scarcely deserve to be called a garden at all . . . much of the magic of the heather beds would vanish if, as we bent over them, there was no chance that we might hear a faint rustle among the blossoms, and find ourselves staring into a pair of sleepy, green eyes."

—BEVERLY NICHOLS, A Garden Open Tomorrow, 1968

When we moved into our house, we had two cats with us, LeRoy and Gray-Baby. We kept them inside for nearly a week after we unpacked. I had read somewhere that cats orient themselves by the sun, memorizing the particular slant of light that means home. I left the curtains open and let them go from window to window, taking it all in: the ocean, the river, the weedy garden, the slightly too-busy street in front of us. By the time they went outside, they knew right where they belonged. They've never strayed far.

LeRoy marked out his territory right away, claiming our entire yard and most of Charlie's. He was a young, wild thing who came to me and Scott in graduate school, after our next-door neighbor Sara gave up on him. "He's a devil-cat," she said, handing him over to us. LeRoy was less than half-grown at the time, with brownish-gray tabby markings and four white paws. How bad could he be?

"You just don't know cats," we said to Sara. "You're a *dog* person. He'll be fine with us." Years later, when Sara came to visit us in Santa Cruz, she let it slip that LeRoy had sprayed her down feather bed. "You can't clean goose down, you know," she said, clearly still irritated.

"He did *what?*" I asked, shocked. "You didn't tell us that when you gave him to us."

"Oh . . . didn't I? I'm pretty sure I did," she said distractedly, bending down to scratch LeRoy behind the ears.

Sara was right about LeRoy, though. He *was* a devil-cat. He had a streak of wild desperation in him that never faded and that we've never been able to explain. During the first few nights we had him, back in Austin, he ran laps through our apartment, beginning at the front door, dashing through the kitchen, into our bedroom, across our bed, often using our pillows as a springboard to launch himself into the bathroom, and back to the front door. I never saw a creature with so much reckless energy. Finally Scott came up with the idea of putting a piece of tape on his tail before we went to bed. He would chase his tail, trying to grab the tape, until he finally fell down from dizziness and exhaustion and went to sleep.

As he grew up, he took to sleeping under the covers, nestled down between the two of us, his head on the pillow. If one of us rolled over in the night, he would stretch out a paw and rest it lightly against us, as if to keep us from moving too far away. It was such a sweet and intimate gesture that it made us forgive him for his wild behavior. In the middle of the night, I would reach over to pet him, and he would awaken and start to purr, then in a minute Scott's hand would find mine on his warm flank, and we would fall back to sleep, connected through our errant cat. He's a couple's cat, we decided. A lover. But by day, he was still a foolish, headstrong fighter, taking on dogs, skunks, raccoons, and cats far bigger and more cunning than he. He always lost and came home sore and wounded and emotionally broken. It took a long night curled up between the two of us for him to be comforted enough to go fight his strange, useless battles again.

He has paid a price for these fights. He wears his battle

scars visibly—torn ears, a bent tail, a scarred nose—and rather than make him look tough, they undermine what little dignity he has. Once he got sprayed by a skunk and came home after midnight, stinking and trying to crawl into bed with us.

When he lived with Scott in Eureka, he got into a fight with a dog. The dog snapped the tip of his femur off, and Scott, who was broke at the time, had to think twice about paying five hundred dollars for hip surgery so LeRoy could get patched up and sent back out into battle. But LeRoy won out, of course, and Scott handed over his credit card, reluctantly, shaking his head over the absurdity of it. The vet saved the little piece of broken-off bone and gave it to Scott in an orange prescription bottle, which Scott rattled at LeRoy when he misbehaved, as if to say, watch out or you won't be so lucky next time.

When we first let the cats outside in Santa Cruz, LeRoy bounded around the yard like a kitten, although he was already five years old, well into adulthood. He chased birds and butterflies, he stuck curious paws down into gopher holes. He caught nothing. Within a few days, he had decided that the yard was his. Whenever I went outside, he acted astounded that I had decided to join him in his world. He scampered up the orange tree and watched me through the branches, his tail waving wildly. He came up behind me when I was down on the ground pulling weeds and put his paws on my shoulders, as if to say, Here I am. Were you looking for me?

GRAY WAS THE EXACT OPPOSITE OF LEROY, and she made it known through her disdain of him. Where he was young and reckless, she was old and wise. Where he was clumsy, she was graceful. Where he begged for our attention, howling and whining and clawing the carpet when we ignored him, Gray sat quietly by, regal as a queen, until we noticed her by her dignified silence alone.

She has been with me since she was a kitten and I was in the third grade. She was my constant companion, waiting in the driveway for me to come home from school, sleeping on my pillow with her head next to mine, following me from room to room, calling after me in her scratchy voice. She anxiously watched me grow up, like a small whiskered mother, circling my bed at night before she jumped into it, her worried eyes following me as I left in the mornings, as if she wasn't sure it was such a good idea to let me out of the house. I thought she would always look after me like that. I never thought about seeing her through old age, becoming the one who would someday take care of her, but of course that is exactly what happened.

She was seventeen years old when we moved to Santa

Cruz. I never thought that she would live long enough to travel with me from Arlington, where I grew up, to my college apartment in Austin, and finally to California, where the fishy sea air and the cry of the seagulls would make her nose twitch and her ears perk up like a young cat. For someone who had lived most of her life in a suburban Texas backyard, California must have seemed like a foreign country. But she adapted as best she could. After all, as long as she was with me, she was home. She even started to follow me outside on the warmest, calmest days, when she could sun herself on the back porch and watch me warily through half-opened eyes.

In her younger days, Gray was a skilled hunter who left headless mice on the doorstep almost every morning in the summer. If she'd been just a few years younger, she might have taken an interest in the birds that were finding their way into my garden; instead, that task fell to LeRoy, who was much less experienced and less cunning. Still, I knew he was up to something one day in early spring when I saw him sitting under the lemon tree, his tail whipping around madly, his eyes focused on the leafy canopy above him. After a few days, I saw what he'd been looking at: a pair of mockingbirds who were building a nest in the higher branches. Every morning for a couple of weeks I got out of the shower, wiped the steam off the bathroom window, and peered out at them, watching them hop around the garden, pick up twigs, and take turns flying back and forth to the nest. All the while, LeRoy watched and learned.

THE MOCKINGBIRDS STAYED CLOSE to the nest or hopped around it, watching LeRoy with a wary eye, charging at any other bird who came near. They established a no-fly zone above our yard. If they spotted a seagull gliding high above the house toward the ocean, they would hop to the roof and screech up at it, scolding it for coming anywhere near their lemon tree.

I worried about those birds. LeRoy seemed obsessed with them, circling the base of the lemon tree, scaring the mockingbirds so bad that they would flutter out of the tree in alarm. But he hadn't tried to go after them, and I'd never seen him kill a bird before, so I watched him only half-seriously, calling out my admonishments from the back porch: "LeRoy, it's a sin to kill a mockingbird."

Then one day in March, I heard the birds shrieking at him, and turned just in time to see him try to climb the tree. I rushed to the tree and pulled him down from the branches, glancing up at the nest as I did. It was barely six feet off the ground. I could have reached up and pulled it down myself.

I took LeRoy inside and dumped him on Scott's lap. "He tried to go after the birds," I told him, my voice breaking.

"What are we going to do? We can't keep him inside until the eggs hatch."

"I don't know . . ." Scott said, stroking LeRoy absently. He got up and went out to the garage, looking for ideas. I followed behind him. After a few minutes of rummaging around, we decided to build some sort of chicken wire fence around the base of the tree. There was only one main branch leading to the nest anyway, so we figured that if we could cut him off from half the tree, we might be able to keep him out of the nest.

I know it must have terrified the birds to see us get so close to their nest, but we worked quickly, and within fifteen minutes we had laced the lower branches of the tree with chicken wire. LeRoy didn't go near the tree again that day, but we had to watch over him for a few days to make sure he couldn't get past the chicken wire. I was starting to act like the mockingbirds, hovering around nervously, always keeping one suspicious eye on the cat.

FINALLY, ONE MORNING A FEW WEEKS LATER, I stepped outside and heard baby birds. It was a creaky little sound, like a door with rusty hinges opening and closing. I couldn't see the babies from the window, but I saw the parents working like mad to feed them, rushing to the ground and back up to the nest, taking turns bending over them. I knew that having me nearby would only make them nervous, but I couldn't resist trying to see the babies. I tiptoed out into the garden and stood on the other side of the lemon tree from the nest, straining to see it through the branches. Both of the adult birds froze in place, watching me with their sharp black eyes, not moving from their perch near the nest.

After a few minutes, the parents got used to me being there and one of them flew to the ground and back up to the nest with something in its beak. All at once, three tiny heads shot up, their necks bent back, their beaks open wide. The bird dipped its head into each of their beaks, then all three babies disappeared as quickly as they had appeared.

The baby birds grew fast. They cheeped almost constantly at their parents, and if a mockingbird can look worn out, these two did. They stopped worrying about LeRoy or about me and Scott tiptoeing over and peeking into the nest from our vantage point on the other side of the tree. It took all of their energy to watch over their three fledglings. They reminded me of the mother in that old Calgon commercial, who is so worn out by the kids and the housework and the phone ringing that she finally locks the bathroom door and sinks into a tub of bubbles, sighing, "Calgon, take me away."

I KNEW THE BABY MOCKINGBIRDS had left their nest when I came home one day and didn't hear their usual cheeping in the backyard. Sure enough, the nest was empty, but the babies were sticking close to home. I saw them, miniature versions of their parents, hopping along the top of the fence, following their parents everywhere and doing their best to imitate their songs.

But my heart sank when I realized that I saw only two of them. I started to look around the backyard, stepping carefully, pulling up clumps of weeds and pulling apart newly planted ground cover. It only took me a few minutes to find a baby bird corpse, half-eaten and cast aside under the lemon tree.

I knew a woman named Jean, who had lost a pet bird. This bird had lived with her for years. It talked to her, whistled at her, did tricks, and perched on her bedpost to watch over her when she took a nap. She left the bird in her boyfriend's care one weekend when she went out of town. He had a cat, but he promised to keep the cat locked in the front part of the apartment and the bird—in its cage—locked in the bathroom.

But of course, the inevitable happened. He came home

on Sunday to find the bathroom littered with bright green and yellow feathers.

It took Jean a while to get over the loss of her bird. But she never could stand to look at her boyfriend's cat again. "I just couldn't be around the cat, knowing that my bird was inside him. It would have been like living with a murderer. You know, he threw up the day after he ate the bird, and I was there when he did it. I kept wondering, 'Is that my bird he's throwing up?'"

I knew how she felt. When LeRoy crawled into bed with me at night, I was convinced he had blood and feather on his breath. I couldn't sleep with him for a week, the little murderer. It was a long time before I could look at him without seeing that dead baby bird.

WE DIDN'T HAVE BIRDS NESTING in the garden again after that. I felt terrible about it; that lemon tree had probably been a nesting site for years. The birds hopped along the fence, looking out for LeRoy, and they only descended into the garden early in the morning, before I let him outside for the day. Over time, I grew accustomed to their quick, rustling departure when I opened the back door in the morning, the sound of air moving and creatures winging vigorously upward, as if the whole garden were flying off.

There seems to be no easy answer to this problem of the cats and birds in the garden. I tried putting bells on the cats, but they voiced their objection by keeping the bells perfectly silent out in the garden, until bedtime, when they crawled into my bed and jingled softly all night long. I have hung bird feeders in high, difficult-to-reach places, where I hoped the birds could land safely out of the cats' reach. And I've often wondered how it is that a cat like LeRoy—a cat with little skill, too many distractions, and foolish pride—could outsmart the quick young sparrows along the fence, much less the scrappy mockingbirds. Once I saw LeRoy running to a shady corner of the garden with something in his mouth, and when I dashed out to intercept his path, I could not believe what I saw in his mouth: a bright blue hummingbird. I grabbed him, roughly, by the scruff of his neck, and his mouth fell open and the bird darted off, unharmed. I was disgusted with LeRoy, but I was a little disappointed in the hummingbird as well. How could such a keen, bright creature get outfoxed by my witless tabby?

The problems with the birds didn't stop me from letting the cats explore my garden. They had been confined to patios and decks for too many years. I was glad that LeRoy had trees to climb, shrubs to hide under, places to explore. Even though Gray didn't go outside much, she found a warm, sunny perch in the backyard, away from the noise and the traffic. I thought that maybe if I planted some catnip I could even entice her to walk around the garden a little bit. Besides, LeRoy loved catnip, and although I still held a grudge for his attacks on the birds, it was time for me to make peace with him.

I found catnip at the nursery in one-gallon containers, full-grown and ready to send the cats into fits of ecstasy. It was on sale, along with some chamomile plants, which were already covered in tiny white flowers with yellow centers. "Steep the chamomile flowers in hot water with a few catnip leaves for a soothing herbal tea," the hand-lettered sign read. Chamomile and catnip tea? That sounded so California, so holistic, so organic. I took one of each plant, and their cheery flowers mingled with each other in my shopping cart as if they were already growing next to each other in the yard.

When I got home, I left the catnip outside on the porch and brought one leaf inside. Both cats jumped to their feet, LeRoy alert and aggressive, Gray shaky and surprised. They followed me around the living room, meowing loudly, until I broke the leaf in two and gave them each half. Gray curled herself around hers and buried her face in it, making small snorting sounds like nothing I'd ever heard from her before. LeRoy ate his out of the palm of my hand, grazing my skin with his teeth, drooling into my palm, grabbing my hand with his paw when I tried to pull it away. I'd clearly found the right stuff. I locked them in the house while I went outside to plant it.

I put the catnip in the back corner of the yard, where I hoped the cats wouldn't notice it for a while. I should have known better, though—when I turned around and looked back at the house, I saw LeRoy sitting in a window, thumping his tail against the glass, watching me with wild desire in his eyes. I dug a hole big enough to hold the roots of the plant as well as the base of a chicken wire cage I'd fashioned from a small section of the roll we'd used to fence off the lemon tree. I anchored the cage around the plant, buried the base of it in the soil along with the roots, and fluffed the plant out, allowing a few shoots to poke through the chicken wire. I hoped that would keep the cats away until the plant got a little bigger. I made the cats wait while I planted the chamomile as well, and before I let them out, I picked chamomile flowers and catnip leaves for my tea.

LeRoy bounded over to the plant, and Gray ambled slowly behind, choosing each step carefully, catching up to him after he'd managed to eat most of the leaves sticking through the chicken wire. Gray gave him a low, impatient hiss, as if to say, Didn't anyone ever teach you to respect your elders? LeRoy backed off long enough for her to come up and nibble a few leaves herself.

I don't quite understand the effect that catnip has on cats. I have heard that it is, paradoxically, both a stimulant and a sedative for them, that it is an aphrodisiac, that it is a hallucinogen. No matter what it is, it made both cats delirious. LeRoy rolled in the dirt around the plant, clutching one wet, ragged leaf to his face. Gray acted as if she'd suddenly fallen in love with chicken wire, rubbing up against the cage with the vigor of a much younger cat. The cage seemed to withstand her affection pretty well, so I decided I could leave them unsupervised and go make myself some tea. I went inside and put some water on to boil, got down a clear glass mug, and poured boiling water over the catnip leaves and chamomile flowers. They looked enchanting, floating there in the water, slowly turning it a lovely pale green. The perfect gardener's drink, I thought.

If I wasn't sure what effect catnip had on cats, I quickly found out its effect—and the chamomile's effect—on people. When Scott came home a couple of hours later, he found the back door wide open and the three of us curled up together in the living room—Gray perched on my pillow, wheezing in my ear, LeRoy sprawled across my chest, his head tucked under my chin—all three of us sleeping off our catnip high.

The Cat's Garden

Catnip isn't the only plant in the garden that cats like. A good cat garden, I have learned from watching LeRoy and Gray, should offer more than their favorite drug. It should provide places to play and hide and things to chase. Here are the plants that I believe the cats would name as their favorites in my garden:

- Catmint: Almost as good as catnip, mildly scented with sprays of blue flowers. Both my cats roll around in it and nibble on the leaves.

- Grass: A few blades of tall grass here and there will settle a cat's stomach and keep hair balls in check. I have even grown a pot of "cat grass" indoors for Gray, since she doesn't get out much.

- Rosemary: Large and shady, this plant provides a place for LeRoy to hide and a good spot for a nap on hot days. And it leaves his fur with a sharp, delicious scent for the rest of the day.

- Fountain grass: Tall, ornamental grasses have a tendency to wave gently in the breeze, and the combination of the motion and the slight rustling sound makes them impossible to resist pouncing on. I've even seen Gray get in on the action when she was feeling good.

Dirt

*You must have a knowledge of soils; must have your soil
analyzed, and then go into a course of experiments
to find what it needs. It needs analyzing—
that I am clear about: everything needs that.*

—Charles Dudley Warner,
My Summer in a Garden, 1870

First gardens are expensive, for all the wrong
reasons. Mistakes are costly; blooming annuals that are so cheap to grow from seed can be very
expensive when purchased from the nursery in one-
gallon containers, but as a beginning gardener I didn't
know any better. I compounded the error by putting the
plants in the wrong location, where they withered from
lack of sun, or too much water, or mysterious soil deficiencies I hadn't yet begun to understand. There is an

old saying that if you have a dollar and a garden, spend ninety cents on the soil and ten cents on the plants, but I hadn't heard that saying yet. I wasn't interested in dirt. I was interested in plants—big, flowering, vigorous plants—and I wanted them *now*.

I spent every Saturday at the nursery, looking for something new to add to my garden. I was a pure impulse shopper; I allowed myself to be swayed by whatever was in bloom when I happened to be there. The sight of all those flowers filled me with a longing too new and powerful to resist, a longing to create something—something of value—out of a patch of earth and a few flowers. I saw my yard as a vast, untouched canvas, and being at the nursery was like being at the paint store, where the colors in the paint tubes are dazzling and the possibilities are infinite. My garden never looked better than it did at the nursery, where I could stand among the plastic pots and imagine it. I bought lavender, Mexican sage, rosemary, snapdragon, and calendula. I hauled cart after cart of plants out of the nursery, convinced that each carload would bring me that much closer to my vision.

I planted the flowers in the side yard where they'd be the first thing I saw when I walked out the front door. I filled four wine barrels on the porch with blooming annuals. I started a vegetable garden of sorts in the back, on the other side of the citrus trees, where I planted broccoli, kale, snow peas, parsley, and cilantro in a little square near the fence we shared with Charlie. Sometimes, if I finished all my planting on Saturday, I'd head back to the nursery on Sunday to buy more.

I had chosen San Lorenzo Garden Center, the largest nursery in Santa Cruz, as "my" nursery, after checking out a few smaller, crowded places on the other side of town and a couple of specialty nurseries that couldn't possibly meet all my needs, one specializing in bamboo and another in begonias. San Lorenzo was the obvious choice, the place nearly every gardener in town flocked to on the weekends. From the outside, it looked irresistible. Big, friendly demonstration gardens around the parking lot were packed with a jumble of flowering shrubs and climbing vines. Flower pots and bags of compost sat out front, along with the redwood garden furniture and whatever racks of plants wouldn't fit inside.

I walked into the nursery every weekend the way a friend of mine used to walk into Tiffany's—helpless, her credit card sliding onto the jewelry counter from between trembling fingers. When I walked into San Lorenzo, the sight of rows and rows of plants, and the flowers cascading from hanging baskets and spilling off the shelves, had the same effect on me. I was beginning to understand how she felt. A person could lose control in a place like this, and I often did. There is no such thing as a budget when you are planting a garden. I followed my heart. I bought *everything*.

The nursery had its own kind of social life, not unlike a cocktail party. People milled around, talking, smiling, looking over the plants the way you might look over a tray of hors d'oeuvres, choosing. And just like a cocktail party, people banded together based on their common interests, clustering around the perennial herbs, squeezing into the greenhouse to look at orchids, gathering under an awning to talk over a new shipment of geraniums. As a newcomer, I pushed my cart up and down the aisles, going from group to group, eavesdropping on conversations, trying to figure out where I'd fit in.

The first thing you saw when you stepped inside San Lorenzo was a blanket of jumbo six-packs, arranged by color like a patchwork quilt. Most of the flowers in the front were quite ordinary: pansies, impatiens, petunias, marigolds. They were tempting, the washes of instant color, but something kept me away from them. I watched the people pushing their carts around them, talking about how to color-coordinate their deck planters with their awnings. Color coordination in the garden?

It just wasn't me. I wanted to join the die-hard organic gardeners, the urban farmers. Never mind that I secretly longed for one of those instant gardens, the kind that you can only get if you buy dozens of blooming annuals, pushed past their natural limits with synthetic fertilizer, and plant them according to one of those generic planting schemes that you might find in the back of a gardening magazine. No, I wanted to belong with the people who had dirt under their fingernails and grew young vegetables with exotic names like *tatsoi* and *mizuna*. This crowd hung out in the back of the nursery, where they picked through the trays of organic baby lettuce seedlings in a knowing way. These were my people. They chose from among the rows of cool-season vegetables that were always accompanied by handwritten warnings scrawled on cardboard signs: "Peas need good drainage during spring rains" or, "Protect parsley in frost-prone areas through the end of March." I didn't have any clear idea how many vegetables I ought to plant for a late spring harvest, or what kinds would grow best near the beach, where it was still cold and windy in spite of the fact that March was half gone. I just took two or three of everything and lined them up in my cart casually, as if I were just getting ready to plant another acre at the farm, as if this was my regular Saturday trip into town for seedlings and provisions. I like to think the other gardeners were nodding with approval, but truth be told, no one even noticed me and my gourmet selection of baby vegetables.

When I left the nursery with my plants, which soon became a weekend ritual, I had to wheel past the pallets stacked high with bags of compost, mulch, potting soil, and manure. I often wondered if I should take the advice of that woman up the street with all the flowers in her yard and buy a bag of compost for my garden. Everyone else was buying it, it seemed. People pulled up in a near constant stream and loaded the backs of their trucks with twenty-pound bags of dirt. I considered it, looking over the bags of steer manure, peat moss, and shredded redwood bark, but I didn't know which one would be right for my garden. Besides, who needed this much dirt? Didn't they have dirt at home, in their own gardens? I decided that these people must have much more important projects than mine. They must have been working on a big landscaping job, or filling planters, or tilling the fields. I got tired just thinking about working all that compost into the ground. Surely I didn't need that much dirt just to plant a few vegetables and flowers.

BUT THE FACT WAS, something was wrong. During those first couple of months, nothing grew much. The little snapdragon seedlings seemed to get beaten down by the wind and rain that was still blowing in off the Pacific. Even the bigger flowering shrubs looked like they hadn't grown an inch, and I began to suspect they were even shrinking a little bit. My yard didn't look like the wild, jumbled paradise I'd imagined, no matter how many more plants I added. Nothing got tall and majestic. Nothing got overblown and blowsy.

I didn't know what to do. I walked around the yard, looking over my frail little charges, worried. One day, Scott came outside and followed along behind me.

"What do you think could be the matter?" he asked.

I sighed. "I don't know. Do you think it's just too cold?"

"Well . . ." I could tell Scott was thinking about a polite way to phrase this. "It doesn't seem to be too cold in everybody else's gardens." He looked around the yard thoughtfully. "You know, when we were kids, my mom always had a garden. I seem to remember us buying a lot of manure for the vegetable bed. Maybe you could try that."

Poor Scott. I had kicked him out of the garden, told him I wanted it all to myself, and now he had to stand by and watch it suffer from my mishandling. I thought about all those bales of compost at the nursery. Could it be that my soil wasn't quite as perfect as I'd thought it was? It certainly looked all right in the beginning. I turned the dirt over during my first few weeks in the garden, when the ground was wet from rain. It yielded easily to my shovel, coming apart in large black chunks. A few earthworms flailed around in surprise. Nothing unusual there, I thought. It looked like all the other dirt I'd ever seen. Why wouldn't I want to plant in this dirt?

It wasn't as if I didn't have perfectly good advice sitting on my own bookshelf that I could have followed. I had a tattered old leather-bound copy of *Loudon's Encyclopadia of Gardening,* published 170 years ago, that I picked up at the flea market. It offered this advice: "The soil of a garden should be in a free, sweet, and rich state, by proper digging, &c. or no great things can be done." Well, I thought, that was a long time ago. Things have changed since then. Besides, those Brits can be such extremists when it comes to gardening. I thumbed through my Sunset book, flipping hastily past the sections on double-digging and raised beds. Boring. Tiring. Dirty. Who needs it?

Well, maybe I did. This "love your garden for what it is" stuff was working out okay when it came to dealing with the weeds, but it began to occur to me that my garden might need more than my careless love. It might need food, too.

What does one feed a garden? I felt like I'd let some strange, exotic animal follow me home, a ferret or an iguana. What does it like to eat? You set out Cheerios, trail mix, alfalfa sprouts. It turns its quivering nose away, offended. You begin to worry that it has gruesome, vulgar hungers that you can't satisfy: live crickets or regurgitated worms. Finally, as a last act of desperation, before the thing dies under your care, you decide to quit trying to figure it out for yourself. You call an expert.

My expert came in the form of a soil test kit that Scott bought for me. I think he was beginning to worry that we weren't going to have much of a garden at all and that I would spend more and more of our hard-earned money at the nursery on plants that would fail to thrive.

I turned the kit over in my hands. The package seemed so helpful, so cheery. Sunflowers with actual smiles on their faces and cartoon nitrogen, phosphorus, and potassium molecules dancing at their feet. "Delicious Vegetables & Fruits," read a caption above a childlike drawing of corn, radishes, and carrots. Happy Houseplants. Abundant Flowers. Yes, I thought. This is what I want. At last, I was on the right track.

The way the kit works is that you dig up a little garden soil, mix it with water, and add a powder to it. It should turn a color—pink, orange, or blue. The darker the color, the healthier your soil. First, I had to get a good sample of dirt. I went out into the garden and looked for fairly undisturbed sections of earth, then dug down a few inches until I hit untouched soil, ground that I had not planted into. This, the directions explained, would establish a sort of baseline. I mixed the soil with distilled water and allowed it to sit overnight until the dirt settled to the bottom of the container and the water was almost clear and ready to test.

Scott came into the kitchen to see the test results. I filled three boxes, one each for nitrogen, phosphorus, and potassium, with the dirt and water mixture, added the capsule of powder that came with each box, and waited for the colors to change. We both looked at the clock, and then back at each other, nervously, expectantly, like a couple in one of those home pregnancy test commercials. The color was supposed to change in ten minutes.

We waited. And waited.

Scott broke the silence at last. "Oh, no," he said, shaking his head. "It's worse than we thought."

"Hush," I said sternly. "It isn't over yet." He sat down across from me at the kitchen table, and we looked intently at the cloudy water in each plastic box, then up at each other with raised eyebrows, and back at the boxes.

Finally, the water in the nitrogen kit began to turn a pale, barely discernible pink. I held the box up to the light, squinting carefully to compare the shade of pink with the color chart on the box. It was worse than I thought. My soil was "depleted" of nitrogen and "deficient" in everything else. I was ashamed to read the results in front of Scott. It was like getting a bad report card.

I turned back to the test kit instructions. "Feed your plants a healthy diet," it read. "Correct plant food deficiencies by adding nutrients in the form of fertilizer. Add compost to your soil to make sure adequate reserves of plant food are available before planting vegetables, flowers, or shrubs and trees." Below the instructions there was a chart showing the amount of fertilizer that would have to be added to bring soil from "depleted" to "surplus or sufficient" for each type of nutrient. Since my soil seemed to be depleted of every kind of nutrient on the chart, I decided I'd just get a little bit of everything to feed my garden.

I went back to the nursery and wandered around looking for the fertilizer section, walking up and down the aisles until I found what looked like my clique of serious gardeners, and I decided to buy whatever they were buying. The choices were a little gruesome for a long-time vegetarian like me: Dried blood. Bone meal. Fish emulsion. What does that *mean,* exactly, to emulsify a fish? I didn't want to know. I remembered something that my aunt once said about the tannery where she worked: "The good news is, they use every part of the animal. Nothing is wasted. Even the entrails and the blood get shipped off to make things like garden fertilizer." I guess that's something. If the animal's going to die anyway, best not to let it go to waste. But I was a little confused as I stood in the organic fertilizer aisle surrounded by aging hippies and small-time farmers, all in their Birkenstocks and their "I Brake for Tofu"

T-shirts. These people all looked like vegetarians to me. Didn't the bone meal bother them? How did they rationalize it? They all seemed to shun the shiny little boxes of synthetic fertilizer, the only meat-free alternative. I couldn't figure it out. I felt like my tribe had let me down a little.

Finally, I settled on a large, friendly looking box of Organic All-Purpose Fertilizer, which contained innocuous but suitably organic-sounding stuff: bat guano, earthworm castings, dried seaweed. I couldn't say for certain that no animal was harmed in the making of this fertilizer, but it seemed better than the murky bottles of fish remains that were my only other choice. When I got to the checkout counter, I ordered up a bag of compost casually, as if it was something I did every weekend. I gestured toward a woman loading compost bags into her car.

"The Organic Soil-Building Compost?" the cashier asked brightly.

"Yeah. Two bags." I pulled my car around and waited in the line of people who were loading bags of dirt into their cars. It didn't seem like such a chore anymore, the thought of working the dried organic fertilizer and all that good rich compost into my garden. It seemed like the right way to begin, the thing I should have done first. As I sat waiting for my compost, it occurred to me that a garden must be a very forgiving creature. It will let you patch things up when you can. It will give you a second chance. Good thing, since I was likely to need plenty more second chances before it was all over.

I pulled up to the pallets, and one of the employees loaded two bags of compost into my front passenger seat. They sat up straight as I pulled out of the parking lot, like a short, stocky copilot. I drove home slowly, careful not to tip the bags over, and on the way, the car filled with the good clean scent of dirt. I breathed it deeply all the way home, and it was rich and familiar and satisfying, like the smell of bread baking, like the smell of the garden itself.

Sheet Composting

I learned, a little too late, that there is a lazy person's way to improve the soil and keep weeds down at the same time. I could have used this technique in the beginning, but now I'm making up for lost time by trying it on one section of my garden at a time each fall.

The trick is sheet composting, which works like this:

Whack the weeds down to a manageable level and sprinkle

them with a good source of nitrogen like alfalfa meal or chicken manure. You'll only need a thin layer to help speed up the decomposition. If you were smart enough to test your soil's pH level and you feel it needs some adjustment, now would be the perfect time to add some lime to reduce acid or sulfur to increase it.

Spread a thick layer of newspaper—about eight sheets—over the area. If you have paper grocery bags or cardboard around the house, you can use that, too. Cover it with a three-inch layer of manure, then build your compost pile right there on top of the manure, assembling kitchen scraps, leaves, coffee grounds, grass trimmings, etc. If you're concerned about looks, you might keep a layer of straw or dried leaves on top. Be sure to water regularly so that all the layers are soaked.

If you do this to a small part of your garden at a time, like I do each fall, you can even create a rotating compost pile, letting the materials accumulate over a few weeks' time, then covering it over with straw and moving onto another part of the garden. In fact, this is a great way to make usable compost in a short period of time without having to manage a large compost bin.

To finish the layering, spread another eight sheets of newspaper over the top and cover with an attractive mulch, like bark or pine needles. The weeds will suffocate, the newspaper will decompose, and, if you do this in the fall, the ground will be weed free and ready for planting in the spring.

First Harvest

*By six weeks its heart will have swollen and enfolded itself
in layer upon layer of crisply crinkled leaves, brittle as French
pastry and juicy as a peach. It will be, say, half the size
of a bowler hat and a lot better looking—and in flavour, if you
have paid attention to what I said about chopped chickweed
and groundsel and a scatter of sawdust, it will taste of walnuts
and ambrosia and even, faintly, of lettuce.*

—On growing lettuce, ETHELIND FEARON,
The Reluctant Gardener, 1952

T he compost made all the difference. I fed
all my plants with generous handfuls of
dried organic fertilizer, and I "side-dressed"—I learned
this term from the Sunset book—the shrubs with my
new Organic Soil-Building Compost, going from plant
to plant like Florence Nightingale bringing medicine

to the troops. They looked better right away. Even though I'd scattered the plants all over the yard, with no particular plan or structure in mind, the garden looked a little less chaotic thanks to the smooth dark dirt around every plant. It made the whole place look orderly, tended, cared for. I kept adding to the garden, buying young lettuce seedlings, thin purple onions, and blue-green cabbages. They sat in my newly restored dirt, looking strong and robust and much happier than anything I'd planted in my garden so far. I hovered over them, watering them, looking out for snails, and raking the soil smooth whenever LeRoy walked across it.

The one plant that didn't seem to need any more help from me was the catnip, which was thriving in its chicken wire cage, poking silvery gray leaves out in every direction. LeRoy seemed to spend most of his time hovering around it, but it managed to get a little bigger each week in spite of him. There was also plenty of catmint, which sprawled along the ground and which LeRoy could be seen rolling in occasionally. Gray didn't get outside much to visit either plant, but I noticed that when LeRoy came inside for the evening, she hobbled over to him and sniffed him excitedly, licking him anywhere she seemed to smell catnip, while LeRoy just stood there, letting her do it, with a faintly embarrassed look on his face.

IT WAS ALMOST APRIL. The days were getting longer, and it became a regular part of my evening to walk around the garden and tend to the plants before dark. It was starting to become an interesting place to be. Thanks to the compost, my vegetable seedlings thrived. The salvia and the lavender starting blooming, returning to the healthy state they'd been in when I brought them home from the nursery. The catnip put out a spray of faint pink flowers, and finally, a few Shasta daisies sent up white blooms. The garden still had a long way to go, but there were these little bright spots, these little islands of springtime that cheered me enormously. Flowers were blooming and it was because of me and my good dirt. We had made something grow.

Still, these little triumphs brought with them a whole new set of responsibilities and worries. A growing garden requires skill and attention and I often wondered if I was up to the task. Maybe I wasn't watering enough. Maybe it needed more fertilizer. At night I sometimes woke up convinced that there were pests circling my house like enemy squadrons waiting to attack.

One day I got the idea to cut a few flowers and bring them inside. Even this made me a little nervous: What if the plants reacted badly? What if I sent them into some kind of state of shock and they quit blooming altogether? I also wasn't sure *how* to cut them. Should they be cut at an angle? Is it better to cut the stem all the way down to the base, or could I just chop it off to any length that suited me?

There *is* an art to picking flowers, as it turns out. The gardening books that kept accumulating on my shelf offered instructions on cutting flowers and treating the stems, all of which I ignored at first. You'd think I would have learned from my compost experience that the advice in the gardening books was usually worth following, but it all seemed like so much trouble for just a few flowers.

For instance, there were all kinds of rules about where on the stem to cut the flowers. Carnations should be cut above the node. Calla lilies prefer to be ripped out at the root, then cut to the proper length later. Woody stems like lilacs should be cut at a 45-degree angle and then bashed on the cut end with a hammer so they will absorb water. Hollow stems such as poppies should be seared with a flame to keep the flower from losing the milky white fluid that is, apparently, its source of nutrients. Once inside, the flowers should be kept overnight in a cool, dark spot like a cellar to "harden" them and make them easier to arrange.

Was picking flowers always this complicated? I didn't think so. I remembered picking wildflowers by the lake where my grandparents lived. I pulled enormous grimy handfuls of them out of the ground and ran up the stairs to my grandmother's front porch, where she would find an old jar for them and suggest kindly that we keep them out on the porch so everyone could admire them. They always wilted the next day, but I blamed it on the Texas heat, not on my own flower-picking skills.

So I didn't bother with any of those fancy techniques from my gardening books. What worked at the lake twenty years ago would surely work now, I thought, as I stepped outside with a tall, skinny olive jar and started picking flowers. I didn't even bring a pair of scissors along. When I saw a flower I wanted, one that I thought the plant could do without, I tugged, I bent, I twisted. Somehow, the flower came off. I did this over and over again until I had a jarful of them, all mixed together in a bright, mismatched jumble of deep blues, fiery reds, assertive yellows, and pale, translucent pinks.

The flowers only lasted a few days, not much longer than the ones I picked for my grandmother's front porch. But pretty soon, flowers were finding their way into the house regularly, and eventually, I started paying more attention to the advice my gardening books gave. After all, why go to all the work of growing flowers, only to bring them inside for a few short, doomed days on my kitchen table?

Besides, I didn't want to injure my new plants, just when they were starting to forgive me for planting them in my awful dirt. I went out and bought some flower-cutting gear so I could do it right: sharp kitchen scissors so the plants would heal where I cut them, metal gathering buckets to keep the flowers fresh, and flower frogs to hold the stems in place at the bottom of the vase. I learned to cut the stems at an angle so they wouldn't rest flat on the bottom of the vase and not be able to absorb water. I stripped off all the leaves that would be below the water line. I even added lemon-lime soda to the water once, which is supposed to make them last longer because the sugar provides nourishment and the lemon/lime acid lets them absorb more water. But this may have been taking things too far. I felt a little silly, offering soft drinks to my flowers. What would they need next? A shot of Canadian Club?

I WAS STARTING TO FEEL like a real gardener at last. Those early visions of me in the garden on the weekends, hauling buckets of freshly cut flowers inside, were starting to come true. But I still hadn't had a single meal from the garden, not one pea, not one onion, not one leaf of lettuce. After all the work I'd put into the garden, I knew I'd feel more like a real gardener when I actually got to harvest something for the table.

It happened one night when we were in the kitchen making dinner. I was grating cheese for Scott's famous homemade macaroni and cheese and he was rummaging around in the refrigerator. "What are you looking for?" I asked.

"I thought we bought lettuce for a salad," he said. "But I don't see it."

"That was a week ago," I told him. "It got slimy. I tossed it out."

"Oh. Well, do you want to go pick some of your lettuce out of the garden?"

My lettuce. It was a silly thing to get excited over, I suppose. Growing lettuce is a small accomplishment; the results are fleeting, perishable. And I only had one short row to show for three months of gardening: a dozen or so plants, barely enough for two salads. In fact, I almost hated to go after them with my scissors. I'd worked so hard to grow them in the first place. They were like little works of art, these lettuce heads in miniature. It was a shame to snip off even a single leaf.

But I did it, and on the way inside, I found a few more ingredients for the salad: a young purple onion, a few parsley leaves, and even a tough-looking lemon from the tree for the dressing. We were out of store-bought vegetables, so there was nothing else in the house to put in a salad, but that was just as well. I didn't want to spoil the experience. While Scott's macaroni and cheese was cooking, I whisked together olive oil, balsamic vinegar, lemon juice, and chopped parsley and green onions, and drizzled it over the greens. It took no time at all to pull together my homegrown salad. Although it was not quite warm enough to eat dinner in the garden, we took our plates outside and sat together on the back porch steps, where we ate our salads in a kind of appreciative silence. It was a small miracle, the first salad from the garden, and it was every bit as good as I thought it would be, crisp and wild and green.

Weed Salad

A true California baby green salad is a work of art. It contains few ingredients because the lettuce is the main event, not merely a place holder for chunks of tomato or cucumber. Here in northern California, we like our salads to be both simple and unusual. Flowers, roadside berries, and even weeds are popular salad ingredients, as long as they are labeled organic and drizzled in balsamic vinaigrette.

Dandelion and wild arugula grew naturally in the lettuce bed my first year, so it didn't take me long to learn to love them in my salads rather than do battle with them in the garden. I even went so far as to introduce a new weed to my garden—a cultivated variety of purslane, a low-growing succulent with thick, crunchy leaves.

Scott calls them my "weed salads," these piles of spiky young greens. But isn't eating one's enemy for dinner the best revenge? Here is my recipe for a wilted dandelion salad, perfect for spring or early summer, when the dandelions look as if they might take over.

> ½ cup walnut pieces
> 3–4 tablespoons extra virgin olive oil
> 2–3 tablespoons balsamic vinegar
> 1 clove garlic, chopped
> 1 blood orange or grapefruit, sectioned and peeled
> dandelion greens, enough for two salads

Toast the walnut pieces under the broiler until lightly browned, and remove. Heat the olive oil over medium heat in a large sauté pan, add the garlic and simmer until translucent. Add the balsamic vinegar and allow it to cook until it is reduced slightly, about 2–3 minutes.

Remove the pan from the heat and add the dandelion greens all at once, stirring quickly to coat the leaves with the dressing, and heat them enough to bring out their bright green color. Arrange the greens on a plate, top with sectioned fruit and toasted walnuts, and serve immediately.

Seeds

*My garden is an honest place. Every tree and every vine
are incapable of concealment, and tell after two or three
months exactly what sort of treatment they have had. The sower
may mistake and sow his peas crookedly: the peas make no
mistake but come and show his line.*

—RALPH WALDO EMERSON, Journal, May 8, 1843

I t took me a while to get around to growing
anything from seed. I puzzled over the other
gardeners at San Lorenzo who looked over the selection
of vegetable seedlings with a sigh. "If you want some variety, you really do have to grow your own, don't you?"
they said to me as we crowded around the broccoli and
cabbage flats.

"Yeah . . ." I answered noncommittally, thinking, what
variety? Isn't an onion an onion?

But of course it isn't. When I started looking over the seed racks at the nursery, I realized that there were at least a dozen kinds of onions, twice as many varieties of basil, and a brilliant array of tomatoes in yellow, purple, orange, and red. This was a new world to me, these seed packets and the exotic varieties they contained. I bought the seeds of an enormous Italian flat-leaf parsley called *catalogno,* orange Mexican sunflowers called tithonia. I was starting to feel like an expert.

Before long, I found out that the most interesting seeds don't come from the nursery. When word gets out that you have a garden, the seeds just come to you. People collect them from the unlikeliest of places and save them up. By the time I got ready to plant some seeds in my garden, I already had a little collection of them, donated by friends and family. It was a surprisingly international assortment. My friend Penny went home to England and brought me back a handful of enormous purple bean seeds. "I don't know what these are called," she said. "They're very popular at home. They'll grow as high as anything you have for them to climb on." My parents brought me vegetable seeds from their trip to Paris: lettuce, peas, radishes. I kept the seed packets in a shoe box and flipped through them occasionally, studying the pictures on the front, trying to translate the French planting directions on the back.

People have even stolen seeds for me. One friend walked through an elegant British Columbia garden, scraping seed pods into her coat pocket and sending them to me with a mixture of dried flower petals and pocket lint. My uncle collected native wildflower seeds from a coastal wildlife preserve and sent me home with a paper bag full of them.

But the best seeds came from my ninety-year-old great-grandmother, Mammy, who shipped them to me from Texas. I have received some unexpected gifts from Mammy, but I was not prepared to come home one day and find a box waiting on my front porch that held a small, ripe tomato and a note, typed in capital letters on her old typewriter, with a few crucial letters missing and ellipses as the primary punctuation:

> TH1$ L1TTLE TOMATO WA$ GROWN 1N HOLLAND, 1 TH1NK 1N A GREENHOU$E. THERE WERE $1X . . . THREE DOLLAR$ AND TH1RTY N1NE CENT$. THEY ARE NOT VERY TA$TY . . . QU1TE M1LD AND A L1TTLE MEALY. THEY WERE $UPPO$ED TO HAVE R1PENED ON THE V1NE . . . 1 BEL1EVE THEM . . . GROWN TO BE $H1PPED TOO. TH1NK THEY WOULD BE REAL TA$TY 1F EATEN NEAR THE $OURCE . . . $QU1$H THE EED OUT ON NEW$PAPER TO DRY AND $EE 1F YOU CAN PROPAGATE THEM.

I called her the next day to find out the rest of the story. She had bought a bag of them a month earlier from her local grocer, she told me, where they hung above the produce aisle in plastic "Grown in Holland" bags. Each bag held five or six tomatoes still attached to a piece of vine (she enclosed the vine also). She took them home and ate them for breakfast, sliced on toast, but she was so disappointed in the flavor that the last one sat in her kitchen for a few weeks, holding its color and texture as if it were made of plastic.

"Then last week," she told me, "I was on the phone with your mother and saw that tomato sitting by itself on the counter. Its brothers had all been eaten by then, so I said, 'I just might send that tomato to Amy!'"

Yes. This is what Mammy does. Sends a tomato halfway across the country rather than throw it out. When a tomato arrives from Mammy, it is more than a tomato— it is a set of instructions on how to live. It is her way of communicating to me: Be frugal and practical, but also be creative. Take the smallest seed from the most ordinary fruit and make something of it. She encourages these qualities in me, and that is her special gift as a great-grandmother. What could I do? I cut the Holland tomato in half, squeezed out the seeds, and spread them out on newspaper to dry, each seed suspended in a little globule of pink tomato jelly. I got an envelope out and labeled it "Mammy's

Holland Tomatoes," and I vowed to plant the seeds in my garden and send her the firstborn come summer.

There were other seeds, seeds I had bought at the nursery, seeds I picked up at the drugstore for ten cents a pack when their expiration date had passed, and a bunch of vegetable seeds that I ordered from a catalog. It amazed me how different they all were. Chamomile seeds were as small as dust, so tiny that I didn't even really plant them, I just scattered them on the surface of the dirt. Lavender seeds were small, too, exactly the size and color of fleas. On the other end of the spectrum, there were Penny's enormous English beans and purple hyacinth beans, which I ordered from a catalog and could hardly bear to plant, I was so charmed by the round brownish-black seeds with the white stripe that ran through each of them like the filling in an Oreo cookie.

I never got used to opening a package of seeds and finding a handful of food inside. It seems obvious enough that you'd plant sunflower seeds to grow sunflowers, but it wasn't until I opened a package of Mammoth Greystripe and shook a handful of gray-and-white-striped seeds into my hand that I thought, Hey, this is a snack food! I'm putting *this* in the ground? The same was true of pea seeds, which are, of course, nothing more than dried peas. Same with beans. Same with corn. I felt like a pioneer woman who had picked and dried the summer's harvest, put it away for the winter, and saved back a few of everything for next spring's planting. Except, of course, that I did no such thing. I ordered mine through the catalog of a seed company in Connecticut. I put them on my credit card.

I CHOSE A SUNNY DAY in mid-April for seed planting day. I was a little nervous that I'd waited too long to plant some of the spring crops, like peas and spinach. And some of the seeds, particularly the tomatoes, came with instructions to start them indoors six to eight weeks before the last frost date, then plant them outside. But we didn't have any frost in Santa Cruz. And I didn't have a place to start them inside.

I tried not to worry about any of that. I had amassed a couple dozen seed packets, and now I had a big square vegetable bed dug. My lettuce was full-grown; my herbs were still thriving. I had eaten most of the onions before they'd gotten very big. I decided to just scratch the seeds into the ground next to the vegetables I'd planted before. What came up, came up. What didn't, didn't. So be it.

It took a surprisingly long time to plant all my seeds. I had been collecting labels from the plants I bought at the nursery so I could use the backs of them as row markers.

To plant a row, I would begin by writing the name of the plant on the label in green marker, then I'd read the directions on the package to try to figure out how deep I should plant the seeds and how far apart. In general, the bigger the seed, the deeper you plant it. The tiniest seeds, the ones no bigger than flakes of black pepper, get sprinkled onto the ground and watered just enough to push them into the dirt a little ways.

The issue of spacing was a little more troublesome. I knew that no matter how carefully I spaced my seedlings, they would have to be thinned later to allow each one enough room to grow. In fact, I had just recently delivered a lecture to my friend Annette in Albuquerque on that very subject. I had sent her a can of wildflower seeds for her new garden and she called asking for advice. "It says on the can that I have to thin them," she said, worried. "Does that mean rip them out? All my little seedlings I worked so hard to plant? I have to *murder* them?"

"Yes," I told her, trying to sound strict and authoritative. "It's for the good of the plants. If you don't thin them out, none of them will have room to grow and they'll all die. So get out there and do what you have to do." As Annie Dillard said, are you a woman or a mouse?

To be honest, I felt like a mouse, out there with my seed packets, glad that Annette wasn't around to see how much

I was dreading having to follow my own advice. Maybe, I thought, if I'm very careful with the spacing, I won't have to thin a single plant. After all, how could I waste any one of those seeds, those beautiful, zany seeds?

So I tried to space them perfectly. It wasn't easy. The carrot seeds had to be a half-inch apart. The tomatoes had to be eighteen inches apart. One kind of bean needed six to ten inches of spacing; another, almost identical bean only needed four inches. The chamomile was impossible to spread evenly.

It was good, honest work, kneeling in the garden with the sun on my back and the dirt warm and dry under my knees. I marked each row carefully with the seed markers and smoothed the soil over the seeds as if I were tucking them into bed. By the time I finished, the sun was going down, and I sat back on my heels to survey my work. My eyes traveled across the smooth, turned vegetable beds mounded with black soil, the seed markers in straight rows around the edges. All that rich, fertile ground, just barely concealing hundreds of seeds, many from faraway places. It seemed so full of possibilities.

As I sat admiring my vegetable patch, I was struck, all at once, by how simple gardening looked. So easy. So obvious. Pull the weeds, turn the earth, mark a straight line, and drop some seeds in. Water. Wait. In a few weeks, the fat bluish-green seed leaves will emerge. A few weeks later, a set or two of true leaves will appear, and sometime after that, a full-fledged carrot or radish, ready to be picked and brought inside. What could be easier? What, really, is all the fuss about?

This quiet place seemed so far removed from the stacks of gardening books that were piling up next to my bed, each one describing ten different ways to stake your tomatoes and another ten ways to support your pole beans. And then there were the complex crop rotation plans, the lists of flowers that will attract the good bugs and repel the bad ones, and lengthy descriptions of all the tools a gardener needs: different pruning shears for different plants, shovels, rakes, dibbles, trowels. I go to a great deal of trouble to do a very simple thing, I realized. I hover over it and worry about it all the time. I'd been spending hours each month at San Lorenzo trying to figure out what to add to my garden, what plant or product I needed to buy to improve it. I'd bought tools and gloves and even special gardening shoes.

But gardening is about none of that, really. Strip away the gadgets and the techniques, the books and the magazines and the soil test kits, and what you're left with, at the end of the day, is this: a stretch of freshly turned dirt, a handful of seeds scratched into the surface, and a marker to remember where they went. It is at the same time an incredibly brave and an incredibly simple thing to do, entrusting your seeds to the earth and waiting for them to rise up out of the ground to meet you. Looking out over the rows of finely sifted black earth, planting a garden suddenly seemed like the easiest, most natural thing I'd ever done.

Seed Catalogs

In her journal *The House by the Sea*, May Sarton writes, "What an excitement it is to order rosebushes in this glacial world, and also to read the seed catalogs by the hour, slowly coming to decisions!"

Seed catalogs not only offer the best variety, they are great company when winter rolls around, or even on summer evenings when it is too dark to work in the garden any longer. If not for the catalogs, I would have never discovered these interesting varieties:

- *Freckles lettuce,* described by one catalog as a "Jackson Pollock take on romaine" because of the dark red splotches on its leaves. I grow it alongside Lollo Rossa, a deeply ruffled lettuce with lovely dark rose coloring at the tip of each leaf. They make a spectacular red and green salad when they're picked together.

Scarlet runner beans, the enormous purple beans that Penny smuggled back from England. These pole beans have started to turn up in seed catalogs more frequently, and they're prized for their bright red flowers, which attract hummingbirds and can be eaten in a salad or used to flavor goat cheese. The green beans are delicious when picked young and steamed. Late in the summer, when the pods have gotten long and fat, I cut them into one-inch pieces, sauté them in a little olive oil and butter, and season them with fresh dill, salt, and pepper.

Golden beets and Chioggia striped beets will make a beet lover out of anyone who grew up hating those glistening red slices at the steak house salad bar. Golden beets have a mild taste and don't leave a dark red stain on everything. The striped beets have a red and white bull's-eye pattern when you cut into them. Scott's favorite fall meal is golden beet risotto, made with both the beets and the young beet greens, and we know it's spring when we're eating thinly sliced striped beets on top of our salads every night.

🌺 ***Pinwheel marigolds*** made a marigold lover out of me again, after I'd scorned them for years as short, stupid bedding plants. These orange-and-red-striped marigolds grow up to four feet tall and, when I don't pick them all to arrange with zinnias and sunflowers, they attract good bugs like ladybugs to the garden.

Compost

*You may begin with a simple bit of leaf-chasing and before you
know where you are you are following a milkman's horse round
the streets with a bucket and shovel or talking bio-chemistry with
ancient bearded ladies, ancient bald men and the intense young
of both sexes, while being allowed to turn their compost heaps
as an especial Sunday afternoon treat.*

—ETHELIND FEARON, The Reluctant Gardener, 1952

No matter how much I expanded my vegetable garden, I always left one row empty
—the row in the middle where snails had nibbled my
first crop of lettuce to the ground. I can't explain why,
exactly. I guess I worried that the original spot was
cursed, that the rotting corpses of those failed plants
would discourage anything I tried to plant next. It hadn't
occurred to me yet that compost was nothing more than

the dead bodies of old plants. Who would have guessed that a plant could survive—even thrive—on the slowly decaying remains of its ancestors?

But my plants *were* thriving, thanks to all the compost I was bringing home from the nursery. Before long, I wanted to try making some myself. Buying it in bales from the nursery was getting expensive, and besides, I had decided that real gardeners didn't buy their compost; they made their own. It seemed fitting that the garden should take care of itself, that last season's mistakes and excesses would become this season's mulch. And it seemed so simple. Arrange your garden clippings into a pile, stand back and wait. Sooner or later, it will disintegrate—everything does—and become compost.

I already had a pile behind the lemon tree where I had been dumping weeds and dead leaves since we moved in. Whenever I worked in the garden, I gathered up everything I yanked out of the ground and added it to the pile. I didn't know much about the science of composting, but I knew one thing: no matter how much I put on that pile, it never got much bigger. Something was happening, deep in the slop of sticks and weeds, something mysterious and altogether new to me.

After a while, I started saving kitchen scraps to add to the heap. Every time I peeled an onion, chopped the green top off a carrot, or picked the outer leaves off a head of romaine, a pile accumulated on the counter. I tossed it all into a bucket on the back porch, and once every few days, I emptied the bucket onto the pile behind the lemon tree.

Still, nothing in that heap resembled the dark, crumbly stuff I bought at the nursery. It looked more like a pile of trash that I'd been too lazy to throw out than something a sane person would deliberately choose to make a part of their garden. I began to do some reading and before long I realized that I had made some serious mistakes with my first compost pile. I had built it almost entirely out of weeds whose seeds and roots would remain healthy and viable, making it impossible to spread the compost around my garden without spreading weeds as well. I had stacked it high with gnarled branches and tree limbs that would probably never decompose. I had added table scraps of all kinds, from cheese to pasta sauce to salad dressing. No wonder it smelled so bad. A good compost pile, I later found out, should consist of alternating layers of green and brown organic matter. No weeds. No processed foods. No big, bulky items. It should be turned often to provide oxygen to the entire pile, something I had never done. If I followed these instructions, the books assured me, my compost pile would not attract flies. It would not smell like garbage. It would smell like the forest, and after a few months, it would offer up dark, rich compost for my garden.

I felt guilty and mildly worried about the unorganized heap that I'd started in the backyard. I became more selective about what I added to it, and I even tried to turn it once or twice, but mostly I just worried about it. I was afraid to tamper with it too much; I thought I might make it worse. It was well into spring before I got around to investigating what was at the bottom of it.

I was out in the garden, checking on things, as I did every evening, when I noticed that my compost pile was smaller and darker than ever. Maybe something really was breaking down inside that pile, despite the fact that I deliberately ignored most of the rules of composting. I decided to find out. I pulled on a pair of gloves and tossed off all the leaves and vines and kitchen scraps from the top two-thirds of the pile, dumping them into a new pile next to the old one. When I reached the bottom, I saw it: dark crumbled leaves, bits of broken-up bark and sticks, and, unbelievably, dark, rich compost. Not much, but at least a bucketful or two.

I turned it over with a shovel and thought about what to do with it. It was full of sticks and twigs, nothing like the finely crumbled compost that I had been buying at the nursery. I started picking the sticks out, but it was slow going. It would take all day to pick my compost free of debris and get it ready to add to the dirt in my garden. I had read somewhere that compost could be screened, so that the larger bits were sifted out and put back in the pile, while the smaller bits could be added to the soil. I decided to try it.

I found an old window screen in the garage, and a cardboard box that could catch the compost after it was sifted. I took handfuls of compost from the bottom of my pile and tossed it onto the screen. Most of the compost slid down the screen, and hardly anything fell through it into the box, but I kept trying, screening the compost the best I could and tossing what remained onto my new pile. When I was finished, I lifted up the screen and looked into the box. About three cups of dirt, fine as powdered sugar, dusted the bottom of the box. Wow, I thought, this is a lot of work for a little bit of compost. But I scattered it around my garden as if it was fairy dust, sprinkling a little of it over my newly planted vegetable seeds, some of it around the catnip, and saving the last pinch of it for the orange tree, which was just coming into bloom and starting to infuse the entire garden with its sweet scent.

CLEARLY, I WAS GOING to have to keep buying compost at the nursery to supplement the meager amounts that my pile at home could produce. But compost wasn't the only soil amendment, I discovered. There was an amazing variety of rich, earthy stuff that I could take home and add to the garden. Over the next few weeks, I must have bought one of everything San Lorenzo sold. I was becoming a connoisseur of dirt. I circled the pallets in the parking lot every weekend, choosing. Peat moss and shredded redwood bark seemed like interesting choices. I bought a bag of each and brought them home just to try them out, admiring the light powdery peat moss, wincing as I pulled tiny splinters out of my fingers after spreading the shredded redwood bark around. That didn't discourage me, though. I wanted to try everything they had.

The manure intrigued me the most. I started out with steer manure, cheap stinking bags of it, only $2.99 for a bag of something so dense that I couldn't even pick it up. They had to load it in the car for me at the nursery, and at home, Scott came outside and hauled it up the stairs, where I dragged it from place to place, cutting a long gash in the bag with my shovel and letting the smell of it waft up around me as I spread it around my plants. It was one of those smells that some people would love and others would hate, not too different from how people feel about overripe cheese.

Chicken manure was lighter in color, fluffier, milder,

more like dirt than manure. Also more expensive, but I could understand why—while I had a pretty good idea of what might be involved in collecting manure from cows, getting it from chickens seemed like a much trickier proposition. They are smaller, and flightier, than cows. It seemed like it would be difficult to accumulate much of it, and besides, I knew what bird droppings looked like, and this chicken manure had undergone some sort of transformation from its original state.

Then one day, a new kind of manure appeared at the nursery, in bags not much bigger than bags of potato chips, priced at twelve dollars, and full of—I'm not kidding—earthworm castings. I stood staring down at it, too amazed to pick it up. "Black Gold," the label said. "The Very Finest for Your Garden." *Earthworm* manure? How did they do that? I tried to imagine the process for collecting earthworm castings. The only image I came up with was something in a laboratory, something with lots of glass tubes and worms slithering around inside, similar to an ant farm, maybe.

I was curious to know what earthworm manure could do for my garden, but I couldn't bring myself to spend twelve bucks to find out. I worried that I would get it home and never get around to using it, like the bottle of very expensive bubble bath that collects dust in the medicine cabinet because it is too fine to waste on an ordinary bath. But I couldn't get the worms out of my mind, so I began to do a little research. I found out that earthworm castings were actually what remained behind after earthworms worked their way through a compost pile, slowly digesting and leaving behind the rotting leaves and scraps. People built special boxes just to house their worm communities. There was even a name for it: *vermicomposting.*

I saw a worm composter for the first time on the student farm at our local university. It was a homemade thing, patched together out of old boards and wooden packing crates. A cupboard door served as a lid, and when I opened it, dozens of red wigglers squirmed under a pile of rotting lettuce. I lifted off the top tray—this composter was made of three stacking trays—and saw hundreds more sifting their way through crumbling black compost, which was almost the same color and consistency as coffee grounds. It seemed so . . . *farmlike,* to have this little herd of worms to tend. So organic.

Worms have special needs, one of the apprentices at the farm told me. They don't like the rain or the cold. You have to keep lots of shredded newspaper on top of the compost to keep other bugs from getting in there with them. And they won't eat just anything. Their favorite foods are banana and melon skins, and they like coffee grounds. They can't have any fat or processed foods. And they'll eat orange peels or onion skins, but they save them until the very end, until there is nothing else to eat.

Oh, they're picky eaters, I thought. They have little personalities. I *want* them.

A few weeks later, San Lorenzo got a shipment of worm composters and put them out on display. They were smooth, round, and black; they looked serious and high-tech. Three round stackable trays with holes in the bottom and a spigot at the base of the lowest tray for drainage. That's all there is to it. The worms start out in the lowest tray, eating kitchen scraps and leaving their black manure behind. Once that tray is full, they wiggle through the holes up to the next tray. After they have eaten their way through three trays of compost, you take the bottom tray off, add the earthworm castings to your garden, and put the tray on top to start all over again. The spigot at the base of the composter drains liquid out of the lowest tray, making an almost endless supply of liquid fertilizer available for the garden.

It was like an earthworm city, where everyone went to work and ate their dinner and raised their children. I had to have one. The woman at the nursery was so pleased. "Oh, you're just going to love this thing," she said. "We have one in the back. Want to see?" She took me into their storeroom, where they had a composter set up in the corner. She lifted the lid and I peered inside. Dozens of worms swarmed over some coffee grounds and lettuce leaves. "Have they ever tried to escape?" I asked, wondering how far they would get on the concrete floor.

She smiled fondly at them. "No, of course not." Then, leaning close to them the way a doting aunt leans over a baby crib, she added, "You *love* it here, don't you? You wouldn't *leave* me, now, would you?"

Something about these worms inspires affection. "By the way, where do you recommend buying the worms?" I asked.

"The brochure in the composter has a list of suppliers. Good luck," she said, as I hoisted the composter under my arm and left.

I sat in the parking lot and read the "Can O Worms" brochure. I wasn't going home without my worms. As the brochure explained, ordinary garden worms are considered "earthworkers," and they eat dirt, not compost. Only red worms are used for composting, since they eat organic, decaying material such as food scraps. Educational supply companies ship red wigglers all over the country for use in science classrooms, and for about twenty-five bucks, they can ship a thousand worms "to your home or office" within a week of the order. I worked in an office where the mail was opened in a central location and then distributed. While the notion of a thousand red worms showing up in our administrative offices for processing and date stamping was tempting, I needed more instant gratification. I wanted my worms immediately. Having bought a composter, I could not wait even a day to get started. I bought a couple dozen cartons of red wigglers from a bait stand on the way home and set up the composter that night.

The composter came with a "bedding block," a brown brick that was made of compressed cocoa hulls. The brick, dropped in a bucket of water, expands and loosens to form a fibrous bedding material for the worms to get started in. I assembled the composter, filled the lowest tray with the bedding material, and added the worms. They came in little Styrofoam containers with about fifty worms in each container. The worms looked a little anemic, as if they had not been fed particularly well at the bait shop. "Don't worry," I whispered to them as I released them into their new bedding. "No one's going to take you fishing now!" I added a few handfuls of lettuce leaves and fruit scraps from the compost pile and left them to get settled in.

That night, before I went to bed, I snuck out to the bin and turned them over with a hand shovel. They burrowed back under their bedding material to get away from the porch light. "Good night," I whispered to them.

IT DIDN'T TAKE LONG for the worms to multiply and fill the bin, just like the brochure said they would. They got the best kitchen scraps, and all the banana skins and melon rinds they could eat. Now that my garden was starting to produce some vegetables, I fed them the tough, outer leaves of lettuce heads, the oregano stems, the carrot tops. I even gathered up fruit peels and coffee grounds from my office lunchroom and brought them home to them.

It took a while for the worms to generate a tray full of compost, but they did produce a steady supply of liquid fertilizer: part rainwater washed through the compost, part rotten vegetable juice, and part, well, part worm juice. It was this last ingredient that made Scott nervous. "What is it?" he would ask fretfully. "Worm blood? Worm excrement? What?" He didn't like it sitting on our back porch. When I turned the spigot at the base of the composter and drained the worm juice out, he turned away, revolted.

He couldn't even get away from the stuff at work. One day he called me from the office, already sounding tired and defeated, and said, "Stephanie wants to know if you can use some extra worm juice. I told her you have plenty—" but I cut him off.

"Oh, great! Tell her I'd love to take some!"

Stephanie did her best to make the bottles of worm juice

attractive. She used old wine bottles, stuck a cork firmly in, and even decorated the front with "From Stephanie's Kitchen" labels. In spite of all that effort, Scott wouldn't bring the bottles into the house. "They're outside," he said to me when he got home. "And Stephanie says you might want to mix them with water first. They're a little"—and here he shivered in disgust—"they're a little *potent*."

I never thought the worms were gross. In fact, I grew quite fond of them. They were loyal pets, productive and well-behaved. I liked to go outside and lift the lid, slowly, carefully, so I wouldn't startle them, and watch them sift through things, working their way through my cuttings and scraps, leaving only the rich black earth behind.

Worm Juice and Compost Tea

It wasn't enough to feed the garden with compost and manure and bonemeal, I found out. The garden liked drinks, too: murky concoctions full of nutrients, served up in big buckets.

Before the worms came along, I tried a recipe for compost tea that I found tacked up on the bulletin board at San Lorenzo. Let a large bucket—or even a barrel—fill up with rainwater. Cut the leg off an old pantyhose and stuff it full of manure or well-rotted compost. Tie it off at the top, and drop it into the water. Let it steep for a couple of days before you sprinkle it around the garden.

I quit using the pantyhose after a while and just dumped a few handfuls of manure into a bucket whenever I had some to spare. If I was at the end of a bottle of liquid fertilizer, I rinsed it out in the bucket as well. That way, there was always something on the back porch brewing for the plants.

Worm juice and compost tea are excellent sources of micronutrients and provide steady, low levels of the major nutrients—nitrogen, phosphorus, and potassium. As long as it is diluted to the color of weak tea, these garden cocktails will not burn plants. Wait until early evening when the sun will not scald the leaves, and pour a bucketful over the entire plant, leaves and all, to help prevent fungal leaf-spot diseases and to maximize the absorption of the nutrients.

Oranges and Roses

If your trees are badly scaled over, and half-dead, it will never pay to try and save such trees; dig them up at once and burn every vestige of them. Do not lose a day in this; now is the word.

—*Jacob Biggle,* Biggle Orchard Book:
Fruit and Orchard Gleanings From Bough to Basket, 1906

On a warm April day, I came home from the grocery store and found Scott standing out on the front porch. He looked like he had terrible news. My heart sank. Was it someone in our family? Was it Gray? I was afraid to ask. I just stood in front of him, searching his face for a clue.

He was quiet for what seemed like a very long time. Then, finally, he spoke. "Our orange tree has ticks," he said, with quiet gravity.

I was so relieved that I had to put my grocery bags down

on the front porch and sit down, laughing, holding my head in my hands, shaking all over.

"What's so funny?" he asked, sitting down next to me.

"I thought someone died," I said. "You looked so *serious*."

"Well, I am serious. We have ticks on our tree. You should see them. It's disgusting."

"We don't have *ticks*," I said dismissively. "There is no such thing as a tick that sucks tree sap. They only suck blood."

"Oh yeah? Well, come look."

I followed him around to the backyard, my groceries abandoned on the porch. I stood under the orange tree and looked up at it. "Looks like a regular orange tree to me, honey. Bark, leaves, flowers, and—oh! What's this? Oranges!"

"You think you're so smart," he said. He'd learned that particular rebuke from my mother. I should have never introduced the two of them.

He pulled a branch down until it was eye level with me. He turned a leaf over, touching it as little as possible, as if it were some creepy thing LeRoy had caught behind the garage. "Look," he said dramatically.

I looked. The back of the leaf was covered with little round black things that looked exactly like tiny ticks.

"Eeeeewwww!" I said, jumping back from the branch. I

walked around the tree, looking closely at it from underneath. They were *everywhere*. "What *is* it?"

"I told you—" Scott started to say, but I interrupted him.

"They are not ticks. I'll take a leaf to the nursery. We'll figure this out."

SCOTT UNPACKED THE GROCERIES while I got back into the car and drove to the nursery with a twig from the orange tree sealed inside a plastic bag. The woman at the information booth shuddered when she saw it.

"Scale," she said. "And aphids, and of course ants, who follow along behind the aphids because they like the sticky sweet stuff the aphids leave behind. You might not be able to save this tree. But try this," and she handed me one bottle of pesticide and one of dormant oil.

"Do I really have to use this stuff?" I asked. "Isn't there some organic spray I can buy?"

She shook her head. "Your tree is really far gone. You might lose it no matter what you do. Try this once, and you should be able to stay organic after that."

Each bottle came with a booklet of warnings about how to use the product. Pick a calm day with no wind, so a toxic cloud won't drift into your neighbor's yard. Don't plan on eating food grown on or near the plants anytime soon. Don't reuse the sprayer for anything other than more toxic chemicals.

"What was it?" Scott asked when I got home.

"Scale," I said grimly.

"That sounds bad."

"It is. We have to napalm the backyard. Keep the cats inside."

I ushered LeRoy in and closed the back door. There didn't seem to be much wind. Might as well get it over with. I had a paper face mask, safety goggles, dishwashing gloves, and a fishing cap as protection. I looked like some kind of suburban gardening warrior. I filled up the sprayer with pesticide, attached it to the hose, and turned it on the tree. It was awful work. I had to get close enough to make sure I covered the whole tree, but I also had to keep dashing out from under the branches so they wouldn't drip chemicals on me. I bobbed and weaved, darted in and out, and somehow managed to get the whole tree sprayed. I hated doing it. My garden smelled like a gas station for the rest of the day, but I saved the tree. It put out new growth almost right away and never had a serious infestation again after that.

THERE WERE OTHER OLD PLANTS in my garden that needed help, but I wasn't willing to go to such lengths again. At first they had all seemed charming, so ancient and gnarled, but after the orange tree incident, they were starting to seem like something of a burden, with their strange diseases and nasty medications. The wisteria was in the wrong place, stuck in a corner with nothing to climb on. And the camellia got too much sun, which meant that its leaves turned an awful sunburnt yellow. The mock orange shrubs in front were dull and uninspiring and required constant trimming to keep them from blocking our windows.

But the rosebushes were the biggest problem of all. They were dormant when we moved in and I hate to admit it, but I didn't like them from the start. I just couldn't find anything to love about my rosebushes. The old adage about politics and sausage is true of roses as well: People who like roses should not watch them grow. Those gnarled, thorn-covered branches and mean, prickly leaves looked like some horrible monster that had just crawled out of the earth and colonized the flower bed.

And they were so fickle and difficult to care for! I had already learned to identify whitefly, rust, and mildew, thanks to them. I was afraid to go back to the nursery and find out what kind of chemical warfare I'd have to engage in to save them. The flowers just didn't seem worth the effort. If I want some roses, I'll call the florist and order a dozen.

This was one case where homegrown was not necessarily better.

My neighbor Charlie, on the other hand, had a beautiful rose garden that he had planted for his wife, Beverly—a dozen or so bushes, in shades of red, pink, white, and yellow. After he planted them, he found out that she was allergic to roses. But he still took care of them, pulling weeds, pruning, and fertilizing. He offered me roses every time he saw me, saying, "I can't even bring them in the house, she sneezes so much. Take some."

I adore roses as cut flowers, and will gladly accept a dozen any time Charlie wants to hand them over the fence. Scott brings me roses from time to time, the lavender Sterlings with their wild sharp scent, or tiny antique roses, white with the barest hint of green around the petals' edge. But I neglected my own rosebushes, and over time, as they got uglier and thornier and sicklier, I developed an outright revulsion toward them. The more I neglected them, the hardier they became, the stubborn things. Clearly, they were not going to wither away on their own. If I wanted them gone, I was going to have to take action

Charlie may not have realized it at the time, but the loving care he lavished on his roses eventually led me to get rid of my own. He had pruned his roses months before, in early January, a tradition here along the coast where the temperature rarely dips below freezing and the garden chores continue right through the winter. I watched him with a little pang of envy, wishing that I had the patience and the skill to take care of my roses, or the refined good taste that would allow me to appreciate them. I took careful notes on his technique, hoping I'd put it to good use someday. He worked quickly and confidently, slicing away at each plant with a pair of sharp pruning shears, going back and forth from the rose bed to the garbage can with armloads of thorny branches.

Those pruning shears of his gave me ideas. I had already begun plotting ways to get rid of my roses, but I hadn't come up with the right method. Transplanting? They might refuse to go. Poison? Too easy to hit the wrong plant. No, I needed something easy, quick, and final. I had a pair of pruning shears like his: small, lightweight, easy to handle. The perfect weapon.

I think the roses felt a little nervous around me, like stepchildren left in the care of their evil stepmother. They hunched low to the ground and they tried their hardest not to bloom so as to avoid drawing attention to themselves. They looked uncomfortable and out of place among the plants I'd brought home so far, my natural-born children, the blowsy cosmos and sunny calendula. I'm pretty sure they knew they were doomed as soon as they met me. It was only a matter of time.

Everyone has a time to die. For my roses, that time came one fine May afternoon, when they were at their sickly, thorniest, pest-ridden peak. I got my pruning shears and walked outside, holding them behind my back. It was the kind of day on which no one in their right mind would think to prune a rose, exactly the wrong time of year. Even a beginning gardener like me would know better. I looked around to make sure I was out of sight of the neighbors. I didn't want to arouse suspicion. Without a word, I knelt down next to the roses, lay the blade of my pruning shears against their scrawny green necks, and cut them right down to the ground. It only took one clean cut through the base of the plant, and the whole thorny mess toppled. I threw them over the back fence into the alley, feeling a little like a gardening mob boss, dumping the bodies of those who had become inconvenient. I stood over the stumps and warned them that if they put out so much as a single leaf, I'd be back.

There's something to this murder racket, I realized, as I looked at the bare spot where the rose bushes had been. It felt good. Rubbing them out gave me real satisfaction. Now all I needed was a mob name, like Mundo or The

Shredder. Or how about The Pruner? I looked over at Charlie's roses, innocently blooming in the spring air. I could take them down in a minute. Charlie was out adjusting the sprinklers. Hey Charlie, I wanted to say, in my hoarse Godfather voice, a man can't be too careful about his roses these days. Would be a real tragedy if anything happened to them. A man in your position might want to arrange for some protection.

But I didn't say any of that. Sometimes you need to keep a low profile with the neighbors. I waved, and he waved back, and I went inside, my pruning shears concealed in my pants pocket, the steel blade hard against my hip.

Charlie's Rose-Pruning Techniques

I have to admit that over time, I developed a soft spot for two varieties of roses: Sterling, the icy lavender rose that Scott buys for me, and Just Joey, a voluptuous salmon-colored rose that my hairdresser Jill brings into the shop from her garden. I haven't actually planted one of these yet, but someday I just might. I've kept careful notes about Charlie's pruning techniques, in case.

WINTER PRUNING

Charlie prunes the day after Christmas, but in cold climates, pruning should wait until early spring. Look for branches that have been damaged by winter weather or are old and weak. Using very sharp pruning shears, cut them off from the base of the plant.

Next, look for "suckers," or branches that emerge from the roots and come out of the soil around the plant. Since most roses are grafted onto a different rootstock, the suckers won't produce roses that look like the original plant, anyway.

Identify the main, mature stems, and cut them back to new wood, straight across, not at an angle. You usually find new wood a few inches above the place where the stem originates.

Finally, pick about five strong canes and cut them back to eight or ten inches high. This will help encourage a growth spurt come spring.

SUMMER PRUNING

When you pick flowers, you are doing a kind of summer pruning, so it requires the same kind of care as winter pruning. Charlie and I once watched with dismay as a teenager across the street tugged and twisted at a rosebush, until the shrub was bruised and battered and most of the petals had fallen off the blossom. "Kids," we said in unison, shaking our heads. I never told Charlie that I used to pick flowers that way, too.

Use good, sharp pruning shears and cut straight across, not at an angle.

Be judicious. Only cut a few roses from each plant at a time. If a plant isn't producing well, go easy on it. Let it build up some strength.

Cut off fading blooms as soon as they are spent, so the plant doesn't spend any more energy trying to keep them alive.

If you want large, showy flowers, pick off small buds along a stem, leaving only one bud at the top.

Manual Labor

I woke up on Memorial Day to the sound of shovels hitting the dirt rhythmically, one shovel and another right after it, and then the sound of dirt landing on the ground. I crawled out of bed, quietly, trying not to wake Scott or disturb the cats, and squinted out the bedroom window. Across the street, three men worked in my neighbor's yard. A woman had moved in recently, and so far, she didn't seem too interested in meeting the neighbors. In fact, I'd only seen her once or twice, and this was the first time I'd seen anyone out in her garden. It had only been daylight for a couple of hours, so the crew couldn't have been at it very long, but already her brick-lined beds were cleared of weeds and a pile of dirt and weeds stood in a wheelbarrow next to the garden.

Pay someone to work in your garden. This had never occurred to me before. Through a crack in the curtains, I watched the men work as I pulled on my sweatpants. Their shovels fell into the earth and they lifted them back up, full of rocky soil and tangles of weeds. They dropped each shovelful into the wheelbarrow and continued along the bed, leaving behind a perfectly clean, unspoiled expanse of soil. Five bags of manure sat next to the wheelbarrow, ready to be worked into the earth. They would be finished with her entire garden before lunch.

I thought this over as I stepped out into my own garden, the air still damp at eight o'clock. I had six tomato seedlings in my hands, all purchased from San Lorenzo the week before. The tomatoes I'd planted from seed were only a couple of inches high and growing slowly, so I thought I'd better buy a few from the nursery as insurance. It was nearly June, and the signs at the nursery told me that they were ready to go into the ground and begin the summer growing season. I gathered up a few tools: a hand trowel, a shovel, and a rake to smooth the ground over before I planted. I dragged a bag of compost over to a bed that I had begun to clear a few weeks before.

Since I'd already pulled most of the weeds, I was ready to start working the compost into the dirt. I had heard that tomatoes were hard to grow in Santa Cruz, between the clay soil, the cool foggy summer, and the pests and viruses that plagued virtually every backyard tomato patch. I wasn't taking any chances. I had bought every organic tomato product that San Lorenzo had—dried fertilizer, liquid Big Bloom fertilizer for later in the year, and mysterious powders and soaps that were supposed to prevent diseases that I hadn't even heard of before: blossom end rot, fusarium wilt, septoria leaf spot. I mixed everything up with the compost, spread it around on the ground, and added a little compost that I'd been saving from my own pile; I even worked in a few shovelfuls of earthworm castings from the worm bin. I turned the soil, one shovelful at a time, pushing the shovel into the dirt with my foot and turning it upside down so that the compost would end up on the bottom and the original soil on top.

It felt good to be out in the sun, planting my tomatoes at last. Although there was still a chill in the air, I got so warm from the work that I stripped off my sweatshirt and continued working in short sleeves, panting a little and rocking back and forth as I pushed the shovel into the dirt. My tomato plants sat in a neat row alongside, looking on expectantly, as if they, too, were glad to be outdoors and ready to go into the earth. It was a perfect day for planting. The fog was clearing and a slight breeze brought the smell of the ocean to me. There was no better place to be than out in my own garden, planting the summer vegetables. I couldn't *imagine* paying someone else to do this. It would be like paying someone else to walk on the beach or pet the cats. What's the point?

I planted the tomatoes in two rows of three each and lashed them to bamboo stakes with twist ties. They looked so young and hopeful in their neat rows. They had no idea what they were in for, between the wilt and the fungus and the air raids from aphids. I squatted down to look them over. "Well, troops," I said. "Do your best. I'll be here to help out when I can, but you're basically on your own now. Don't let me down."

The tomatoes planted, I went around front to do some weeding. The workers across the street had already finished their job. They were washing off their tools and getting into their truck as I flicked a couple of snails off a stepping-stone and sat down among a sea of dandelions and nut grass, an entire day's work spread out before me. The men across the street drove off, and my neighbor came out of her house in a spotless white shirt. She walked around the cleared beds slowly, surveying them from each angle. She must not have been out there very long, because when I had finished weeding everything within reach and had moved to the next stepping-stone, I looked up and she was gone.

I COULDN'T IMAGINE doing as much manual labor as my neighbor's work crew, day after day. Pulling weeds and hauling dirt and cutting branches is serious work. In fact, I don't think I was ever prepared for how hard gardening would be physically.

I put my back into this garden, quite literally, straining myself so badly with the bags of manure and the shovels and pitchforks that some days I could barely limp back into the house at sunset. Once, a couple of months after we moved in, I wrenched my back so quickly and painfully that I fell onto the ground I had been preparing and lay in the newly turned earth for a half hour or so, unable to move, staring up at the sky, the clean smell of dirt wafting up around me. This is what it would be like to be a plant, I thought, unable to roll over or turn my face away from the sun.

It seems funny now, looking back, to think of myself stuck in my own dirt, unable to move. But I was terrified at the time. I was twenty-five when we moved into the house, and I had never dealt with a physical limitation like that before. It took weeks for my back to heal, and my work in the garden was severely restricted because of it. I couldn't bend, I couldn't dig, I couldn't lift. As soon as I got back to my regular work in the garden, I injured myself again in the same place. And again, and again.

"If you don't start doing sit-ups every day," my chiropractor told me, "this will never really get better. You'll just keep injuring it over and over again. Let me see you do one sit-up."

I did one for her on the examining table, my whole upper body trembling from the effort.

"See that?" she said. "You won't shake so much after a while. But you've got to build up some abdominal muscles so your back doesn't do all the work for you."

I took her seriously. I was beginning to worry that I would have to stop gardening, which was out of the question. I did sit-ups all spring, starting with ten a day, then twenty, then fifty. Eventually, I was up to a hundred a day. I never got the rock-hard abs that I saw on television infomercials, but I got much stronger. When I carried a bag of compost around, I felt my stomach muscles kick in and hold me in place. My tender, injured back felt safe, protected. Slowly, it began to heal.

Gardening continued to push against my physical limits,

though. I could still haul around only the smallest and lightest bags of dirt. I still had trouble shoveling the beds and I was stiff and sore at night after a day in the garden.

If exercise worked for my midsection, why not my arms? I wondered. Who says I need somebody to help me carry bags of manure out of my car? Why can't I do it myself?

I started doing push-ups and lifting weights—slowly at first. My first hand weights were only two pounds each. But I had learned something from the sit-ups. You work your way up, slowly. I went from two pounds to five pounds, then seven, then ten. It was like the garden itself. Nothing happened overnight.

Then one day, I found myself at the cash register at San Lorenzo, asking for a bag of steer manure. "I'll call someone for you," the cashier said.

"Nah, that's okay," I told her. My mind was already on the gardening chores waiting for me at home. Distractedly, I pulled my car around to the pallets and tossed a bag of manure into the trunk. I was out of the parking lot and three blocks down the street before I realized what I'd just done. The improvement had been so gradual that I hadn't even noticed it. Over time, I had become strong enough to take care of myself in the garden. I had become good at something I had never imagined I'd ever wanted to be good at—manual labor. I could keep up with those guys in my neighbor's gardening crew, I thought. Better yet, I could keep up with my own garden.

NOT LONG AFTER THAT, I had a chance to prove myself right. I worked for a housing agency that found itself in possession of an old boarded up house in a run-down neighborhood near the Boardwalk, just a couple of miles from my house. We planned to fix it up and sell it to a low-income family in the neighborhood. I had no direct involvement in the project, but I occasionally sat in on project meetings to make sure we were following the rules, keeping up with the paperwork, and spending the money on schedule, all the bureaucratic details that it was my job to worry about.

I didn't pay much attention in those meetings. My mind tended to wander in the presence of long discussions about mundane construction details. I used to plan the garden in those meetings, mull over new seed varieties, design a more ornamental lettuce bed, wonder about the best way to stake the tomatoes. Sometimes I'd make a mental list of what was ripe in the vegetable garden and try to think up as many different meals as possible using the food I'd grown: stir-fry, pizza, vegetable stew.

But when talk turned to the little house by the Boardwalk,

I found myself perking up. It was such an endearing project, taking a neglected old house and turning it around. The rehab work was almost complete. It had a new roof, a new foundation, new wiring and plumbing, and a remodeled kitchen. It had been painted a fresh, beach-cottage yellow, and all that remained were a few finishing touches. Like landscaping.

Everyone had forgotten about the landscaping. We had to be finished with the project and the house had to be ready to go on the market in two weeks. Excuses were made; there were confused mumblings about a "landscape plan" or lack thereof.

This is the problem with bureaucracies: Things tend to become more complicated than they actually are. I was feeling a little surly that day, and it probably showed when I spoke up and said, "Oh, come on, how hard *is* this? Go down to the nursery, buy some Mexican sage and some bougainvillea, and stick them in the dirt. This is an eighty-year-old cottage by the beach with a two-foot strip of ground around it. We don't need a *plan*. We need to get some plants in the ground and sell the damn house."

I should have spoken up at project meetings sooner, because the next day I found myself putting on my blue jeans and my old tennis shoes and heading to San Lorenzo instead of the office. I had been promoted to landscaper, just for a day. I pulled into San Lorenzo's parking lot, parked near the front between two landscape contractor pickup trucks, and strode purposefully through the aisles of the nursery, just me and the other landscapers, the only customers who had a reason to be there so early on a weekday morning. I walked around with one of the employees, pointing to plants, making notes on a little notepad, arranging for delivery to the job site.

This is *cool,* I thought, as I handed over my purchase order and left the nursery. People do this for a living. Today, *I* am doing this for a living. I had a work crew showing up at the house to help: Technically, I was not supposed to do the actual planting, since outdoor labor was nowhere in my job description, but I had my garden gloves and a shovel with me just in case it looked like I could get away with getting my hands in the dirt.

I was the first one to arrive on the job site. I sat on the front steps of the house, drinking a cup of coffee, watching for the delivery van from the nursery. This little neighborhood, the Beach Flats, was so close to the Boardwalk that it should have been one of the most expensive and upscale in Santa Cruz. It wasn't. It was a little pocket of poverty in an otherwise affluent town, a tiny neighborhood known for gangs and drugs and cheap motels. From my house up on the hill, I could look across the river and down into the Beach Flats. I occasionally heard gunshots and police sirens in the middle of the night. But for all practical purposes, I lived in another world. I rarely visited this neighborhood on my evening walks, and the Beach Flats residents almost never came to Seabright, except for the man who went door-to-door on his bicycle, selling tamales from an ice chest he towed behind him.

Sitting on the front porch in the early morning fog, waiting for the plants to arrive, I wondered why everyone was so scared of this neighborhood. The houses around me were covered in peeling paint in shades of faded green, pink, and blue; a few front porches were littered with broken patio chairs and discarded car parts; and several windows had been broken out and covered with yellowing posters of *la Virgen de Guadalupe,* but the place didn't feel unsafe because of it, just poor.

Just then, as if on cue, doors began to open down the street. Children emerged, and their mothers or grandmothers followed behind them, carrying their lunches, walking toward the bus stop at the end of the street. They stood around for ten minutes or so, the women talking in quiet, early morning tones, keeping an eye on their children, until a school bus drove up. It stopped for a minute, then pulled away, leaving behind the mothers and the grandmothers, who turned and disappeared, one by one, back into their houses.

I contemplated the scene I'd just witnessed as I finished my coffee. There is an elementary school in my neighborhood, and I have never seen a crowd like that gathered at the school to see their kids off. This neighborhood had something special about it. I looked back up at the house we were restoring. It looked so hopeful, with its coat of yellow paint and its shiny new windows. It looked like it had the power to inspire the rest of the neighborhood to join in and make a fresh start, to mend some stairs, replace some windows, plant some flowers.

The van from San Lorenzo pulled up around the same time the work crew did. I jumped up to help unload plants while the guys went to work clearing the little strip of dirt around the house of the dandelions and blackberries and crusty old aloe plants. They had the weeds pulled and the bags of compost from the nursery spread over the ground, all in the time it took me to help unload the plants and line them up along the sidewalk where I wanted them planted. I pointed and used a little of my high school Spanish to indicate where the plants should go, their spacing from the house, and the need to leave enough room for a picket fence along the sidewalk.

I stood around for a few minutes while the guys started to work, feeling a little silly in my role as plant boss. What was I supposed to do now? Stand there and watch? Give more orders? Go inside and read a magazine? Instead, I did what I'd wanted to do all along: I went to my car, got my gloves and my shovel, and set to work. There were four of us working with our shovels and our pitchforks, but the ground was so hard and dry that it took a good hour or two to work the compost into the soil and get half the plants in the ground.

Around ten, the carpenters showed up to build the picket fence. One of them looked at his watch and nodded in our direction. "Go take a break, you guys," he said, and I dropped my shovel along with the rest of the crew, stuffed my gloves into my back pocket, and walked with them down to the corner store, where we stood out front and drank agua frescas until our fifteen minutes had passed. This is not a bad way to make a living, I thought, although my back was already starting to stiffen up, and I realized with a feeling of something like shame that I probably made double what the highest-paid guy on the crew made, even at union rates. I was playing at being a gardener, pretending that I got to spend my days with my hands in the dirt, but I knew I had a cushy desk job waiting for me, one with a good paycheck and none of the occupational hazards of outdoor labor.

We finished our work before lunch. The guys packed up their trucks and got ready to go on to their next job, but not before they had turned to shake my hand and compliment me on my hard work: *"Eres muy buena trabajadora."* I grinned and shook their hands, too pleased to say much. Before I left, I walked across the street to get a good view of the house and its new landscaping.

The sunny yellow paint, the white picket fence, and the flowers made all the difference. The house was a bright spot in the neighborhood, where before it had stood as a symbol of blight and decay. The plants seemed awkward and new, surrounded by a brown carpet of perfectly raked mulch, but I could just picture how it would look in a year or two, after a family moved in and hung curtains in the windows, after the plants had matured and the entire house was surrounded by the blue and white spires of Mexican sage and purple bougainvillea climbing up a trellis near the front door. Anyone could see that a lot of sweat had gone into transforming that house. And some of it was mine.

Gardener's Bath

Some days, my favorite time in the garden is that hour when the sun has slipped down below the horizon and it is too dark to get any more work done. Nothing to do but put away the tools and retreat inside with an aching back and arms covered in blackberry-vine scratches.

Ah . . . the postgardening bath. It is worth getting dirty for, worth straining muscles for. I bring an alarming amount of debris into the tub with me—there is compost between my toes, a fine dusting of dirt along my arms, and leaves and dried seedpods in my hair. As if that isn't enough, I bring handfuls of fresh herbs into the bath with me, so that by the time I haul my newly scrubbed body out of the water, there will be a trail of fragrant rosemary and lavender buds at the bottom of the tub along with the dirt and the twigs, and a teacup alongside will hold the dregs of my garden tea—catnip and chamomile buds.

Here's my recipe for a postgarden soak that heals my morning-glory rash and soothes my tired bones.

> 1 cup oatmeal
> ¼ cup baking soda

¼ cup powdered milk

dried herbs—comfrey, lavender, eucalyptus, mint, or

chamomile work well

I make a batch of this up in advance by blending everything together in a food processor or blender until it is a fine powder. When I get in from the garden, I sprinkle some into my bath, along with some fresh herbs or rose petals, sink into the water, and—if I have the strength—I start planning next weekend's gardening project.

A Growing Season

Tourists

*We travel, some of us forever, to seek other states, other lives,
other souls.*

—Anaïs Nin, The Diary of Anaïs Nin, 1980

At first, I hardly noticed the arrival of summer. I can't explain why; I guess I was too distracted by the ordinary details of my life to pay much attention. The weeks had a way of slipping by, even in the garden, where I thought the changing of the seasons would be abrupt and obvious. But there was no specific event in the garden that signaled the beginning of summer—my tomatoes didn't all ripen at once, my flowers didn't all start blooming. Up to that point, summer in the garden looked pretty much like spring in the garden, full of half-starts and new beginnings, except that the days were longer and the ground was a little warmer.

Then one day I was driving down Ocean Avenue toward

home, on my way back from the nursery, when I found myself suddenly stopped in traffic. This was unusual—on most days, I zipped right down Ocean, past the dilapidated Victorians and the cheap motels, past the liquor store with bars on its window, past the abandoned cocktail lounge that the neighborhood association shut down, past Freddy's Taqueria and the 7-Eleven. There was hardly ever any real traffic on this street, and I rarely gave any thought to the fact that this was the main road that tourists took to get to the Boardwalk. But this time a long line of cars, barely moving, stretched out in front of me, and without anything else to do but wait, I looked up to the end of the street where the Boardwalk sprawled along the shore. In the distance, I could see the Ferris wheel turning in its slow, grand fashion. The screams from the roller coaster were especially loud because there were two cars running on the tracks at once, and the screams from one car echoed the screams from the other, a half-terrified, half-exhilarated duet that I would be able to hear from my garden when I got home. I realized that the sun was shining, and the stretch of ocean just beyond the Boardwalk was blue instead of its usual gray.

And that's when I realized: *It's summer.* Winter was long over, and spring had faded quickly away, before I even had time to realize it was taking leave. The other cars stacked up behind me and in front of me were full of tourists: tourists with neon pink bikini strings tied around their necks, tourists rubbing tanning oil on each other's backs before they even reached the parking lot, tourists with ice chests in the backseat full of beer and sandwiches. Summer vacation had come to Santa Cruz, and I fell into the role of the grumpy local, irritated by the invasion of loud, boisterous out-of-towners. They parked on my street, they partied on my beach, and they stood in long lines at my favorite restaurants.

Each weekend, they left dirty diapers, beer bottles, and candy wrappers in my garden, and I wandered around in the early Monday morning fog, picking up after them. It was the way they left their trash behind that really bothered me—if they'd dumped it in the street and it had somehow blown into my yard, that would have been one thing. But because our house sits about five feet above the sidewalk, people had to actually *place* their trash in my garden, among the flowers. They lined up their beer bottles in single-file rows next to my geraniums. They tucked fast food cartons under my climbing rosemary. They were deliberate about it. I took it as a clear sign of aggression, as an act of hostility.

Really, though, I think that most of the tourists just never considered the fact that people live in my neighborhood, that we were not part of the tourist attractions, that our street was not an amusement park or even a parking lot. People seemed to feel that we locals were here for them, that we were a paid staff ready to accommodate them. Tourists came to my door and asked to use my phone, and they even tried to borrow gas money to get home. Once I came walking up the sidewalk and found a man pulling an ivy geranium out of Charlie's yard, in broad daylight, *in front of his own kids*. I was so astounded that I just stopped short in front of him, too furious to speak, staring down at the flower in his hand.

After a minute, he smiled broadly at me. "You don't think anybody'd mind if I just . . ." and he hoisted the plant as if he was raising a toast. "We're from out of town— Modesto—and I thought I'd like to try one of these in my own yard."

Was he trying to appeal to me as a gardener? Did he think I'd get excited about how good Charlie's geranium would look in his yard back in Modesto? It took me a moment to find my voice, but finally I said, "Yes, I do think he would mind. He went out and bought that plant, and he put it there because he wanted it to grow there," and I took the geranium from him and tucked it back into the soil, while the man's children looked on, wide-eyed.

People like him made it easy to be a grouchy local. The invasion of privacy, the intrusions upon my home and my life, were not only annoying, they were a little frightening. In a suburban neighborhood, property lines are very clearly defined. There are lawns and driveways and gates, and people know not to cross them. But here, none of us have driveways or lawns or even marked parking spaces. There are none of the traditional barriers to keep the public out. People sit on my front steps to brush the sand off their feet before they get into the car, and usually I don't mind. Sometimes they wander aimlessly up the steps into my garden before they realize that they've gone into somebody's yard. But I really lost it one day when I came home and found a couple of teenagers sunbathing on my front porch—not on the steps, but actually on my porch, right in front of my front door. The man had spread out a beach towel and was sprawled on his stomach, and the woman was lying on her back with her shirt rolled up and her shorts rolled down to expose as much skin as possible without actually getting undressed.

As usual, I was too astonished to speak. They both had on sunglasses, so I wasn't even sure if I was making eye contact with them.

"Hello," I said, thinking I would try the polite approach.

They both looked up at me, said hello in response, and lay back down.

This was too much. I knelt down next to the man and said, "This is my house. It's not a public area. This is like you lying on my front lawn."

The man looked around for a minute, surprised. He looked up at me, and at my front door behind me. He turned and glanced at his girlfriend. "Whoa," he said at last, rolling off his beach towel. They both jumped up as if they had just noticed for the first time that the beach was actually another block away, and they ambled off without another word.

IN SPITE OF THEIR BLUNDERING WAYS, I have to admit that I was a little fascinated by the tourists. They put on their own show, arriving with their beach umbrellas and their acoustic guitars, ready to live the idealized summer fantasy, the beach vacation. While the rest of us went on with our daily routines, scuttling to work and back home again, folding laundry, and paying bills, they turned our usually cold, foggy little town into a beach party that lasted from June to September. They got sunburnt, they drank margaritas, they bought silly souvenirs. In short, they reminded me of myself when I went on vacation. Because of that, I found it hard to stay mad at them.

I could walk along the beach and see replays of every summer vacation I'd ever taken. Toddlers raced up to the shore, shrieking with delight, running back to clutch at the legs of their parents. Young girls rolled in the sand, pretending to be mermaids. Teenage girls propped themselves up on lounge chairs, listening to the radio, and boys showed off on their surfboards.

Occasionally I'd catch a glimpse of some ideal summer romance unfolding at the beach, the kind that everybody wishes for, the kind that only happens in the movies or, apparently, in Santa Cruz. One day in late June, I went down to the beach. The day was unusually warm, with clear skies, none of the typical afternoon fog, and a perfect surf that erupted into gorgeous, foamy, breaking waves up and down the shore. The sun, which was just about to set, cast a deep golden light over the beach. As I walked from one end of the beach to the other, the light caught the spray coming off the waves, framing everyone near the water in a sort of misty halo. A young couple, silhouetted against the sunset, played Ping-Pong in the sand. When the ball went into the water, the woman dove in after it, and the man chased her, until they were both running in the waist-high surf. He caught up with her and grabbed her around the waist, swinging her around and kissing her until the waves receded and they both dropped into the sand, like Burt Lancaster and Deborah Kerr in *From Here to Eternity*.

These people think that such moments are only possible in a place like Santa Cruz. But as a local, I have figured out that it just isn't so. The tourists bring their own magic with them. It isn't about this place. It isn't really the ocean or the sand that makes them happier or funnier or more romantic. I walk along this seashore every day, often with Scott, and we have never dropped into those waves for a passionate kiss in the surf. It is the act of being on vacation itself that makes them happy and relaxed and fulfilled for one short week a year. It would happen to me and Scott, too, if we went to a different beach, in a different town. But the tourists don't know that. They give all the credit to Santa Cruz, and I let them.

And so, over time, I began to want to perpetuate the myth, to be a part of the bright, flowering backdrop to their beach vacations. I thought back to the vacations I'd taken to resort towns and tropical islands, where I looked on with envy as the locals laughed from their front porches, gathered hibiscus and bird of paradise from their gardens, and walked the streets of their thatched-roof villages in the evenings with a familiarity that made me ache with envy. This is part of the vacation experience, watching the locals from a sidewalk café or a sandy beach bar, sipping some tall, sweet drink that would seem entirely frivolous back home, and having a long, rambling conversation with the person sitting next to you that goes something like, "If only I lived here . . ." and drifts to, "See that little white house on the hill? I was *meant* to live in that house . . ." and ends, in a slurred speech, with, "Tell the neighbors they can keep my furniture. Call the office and tell them I quit. All I need is a beach chair and a barbecue grill."

I have had that conversation myself more times than I can remember. But I never thought I would hear a woman say this as she walked past my house: "Look at that sweet house with the red geraniums, honey. Did you know I've always wanted to live in a little cottage by the sea with red geraniums in the front?" And, as they got in their car to head back to San Jose or Fresno or Barstow, I heard him reply, "I know you do. And as soon as we win the lottery, this is where we're coming."

People would trade in their lottery winnings for my house? Could that be true? People felt about my house the way I felt about houses in Carmel or Mendocino or Hawaii? I found it hard to believe, but I was pleased nonetheless. In fact, it was that remark that spurred me on to live up to the tourists' romanticized notions of Santa Cruz. I started growing all the classic California beach plants in my garden. I planted bougainvillea and Mexican sage, the same planting scheme I'd chosen for the house in the Beach Flats. I put in ice plant, the succulent sand dune flower that blooms iridescent pink and purple flowers for one month in the summer. I let trumpet vine ramble around the corner of the house, its red flowers so large that a hummingbird could disappear completely inside one open blossom, and I smiled indulgently when young women reached up and plucked the flowers for their hair.

I did all this because of the tourists, in spite of the noise and the traffic and the garbage that they brought along with them. I was willing to let them believe that this place held the key to their happiness, this town by the sea where the flowers bloom all year long. They reminded me to enjoy my life as a local. I felt their approving glances as I tended my bright seaside garden, and I waved to them from my patio, where I often sat in the evening with a glass of wine. And on Monday mornings, after they'd gone, I walked up and down the street and collected their empty bottles of suntan lotion.

What's the Name of That Plant?

I'll buy anything on vacation. Silly souvenirs, amateurish watercolors, and even those themed cookbooks like the *Spicy Caribbean* cookbook I brought back from the Virgin Islands, all in the hopes of re-creating the vacation experience at home. But when I get them out of the suitcase, these trinkets seem foolish and out of place.

The Santa Cruz tourists are smarter. They are always stopping and asking me the names of plants that grow in my yard, in hopes of re-creating the seaside experience back at home. A surprising number of beach plants grow all over the south and the west, and with a few seashells scattered around the garden, you might just be able to hear the ocean from your own backyard.

The numbers next to these plants represent the *Sunset* climate zones where the plants can be grown. In general, most of these plants can tolerate light frost, but would have to be covered or brought inside for a heavy freeze.

> *Tropical hibiscus,* a flowering shrub that attracts humming-
> birds and grows well in containers or in the ground (9, 12,
> 13, 15, 16, 19–24)

- *Bougainvillea,* the climbing vine with papery flowers in purple and red (22–24, can survive light frost in 5, 6, 12, 13, 15–17, 19–21)

- *Passion vine,* a rambling vine that can cling to netting or a trellis, with red or purple/white flowers (5–24, depending on species)

- *Trumpet vine,* a vine that hummingbirds love, in red or purple (all zones, depending on species)

- *Echium Pride of Madeira,* a shrub with outlandish spikes of purple flowers that grow over six feet tall, bringing to mind a cross between a tropical paradise and a Dr. Seuss drawing (14–24)

- *Mexican Sage,* a salvia with long blue and white spikes of flowers that attract hummingbirds and make great additions to bouquets (10–24, cut to the ground in winter)

- *Fuchsia,* a shrub that grows well in hanging baskets, with purple, pink, or red flowers that have an otherworldly beauty (2–9, 14–24 depending on species)

- *Red-hot poker,* a shrub that is often mistaken for aloe, with tall, fiery red and yellow spikes (1–9, 14–24)

- *Aloe,* often seen growing at the beach, puts out orangish-red spikes of flowers (8, 9, 12–24)

Insects, Good and Bad

The operations for destroying insects, or counteracting their
injurious effects, are our next consideration. These are so
numerous that, were we to enumerate all that have been
recommended by writers on agriculture and gardening, it would
excite astonishment that all the races of injurious insects had not
been exterminated long ago; or, at least, that any should appear
in such an undue proportion, as to baffle our own immediate
efforts to subdue them.

—Jane Loudon,
Loudon's Encyclopadia of Gardening, 1830

When I started gardening, I had no idea that
I would get so intimate with the lives of
bugs. I paged through the full-color gardening books at the
bookstore and I never saw a single bug in any of those gardens. Insects didn't seem to be a particularly desirable

thing to have. None of my favorite gardening magazines ever had a garden on the cover that was swarming with bugs. And I never heard anyone praise a garden by saying, "You won't believe all the bugs she's got out there! It's spectacular!" A garden, it seemed, should be neat and clean and free of insects of all kinds.

But this was never the case in my garden. After that first infestation of aphids and scale on the orange tree, I started paying more attention to the bug population in my backyard. I did a little reading, too, and found out that organic gardeners divide the insect world into two camps: good bugs and bad bugs. The bad bugs bring death and disease and destruction to the garden, sucking the life out of crops, infesting the soil, and laying eggs by the thousands. The good bugs swarm in like handsome, broad-shouldered NATO peacekeepers, bringing peace and justice and harmony. They watch over the crops, and while you're not looking, so as not to frighten or disturb you, they munch discreetly on the bad bugs.

One of the first things I noticed was that the good bugs were all prettier than the bad bugs. Or at least the photos in my organic gardening books made it look that way. The good bugs, the hover flies and the ladybugs and the honeybees, were always photographed in the center of a bright pink dahlia or a sunny yellow zinnia. They all had adorable stripes or dots or elegant, lacy wings. They looked like the sort of bugs you'd want to have in your garden. They were friendly and cheerful and not at all creepy.

The photos of bad bugs, on the other hand, made my skin crawl. Whiteflies swarmed over the underside of a tomato leaf. The squash vine borer larvae, a sickly white grub, chewed through a tough old squash vine. Armored scale rose along the bark of a tree like pimples, swollen and faintly purplish. Even the Mexican bean beetle, which looks almost identical to a ladybug except that it is copper colored instead of red, was photographed in a dim, greenish light that made it look vile and corrupt.

The good bugs also got better names, some fierce and warlike, others graceful and feminine. Who wouldn't want a spined soldier bug, a robber fly, or a minute pirate bug on your side? Or a ferocious tiger beetle, or an ant lion? And some of them sounded so lovable: damsel flies, lacewings, lady beetles. The bad bugs, on the other hand, all had names that sounded like the kind of things little kids would call each other on the playground: cabbage maggot, canker-worm, stink bug. The lines were drawn, and they were fixed and firm. The insect guides were as reassuring as fairy tales, where the good guys are distinguished sharply from the bad guys, and good always triumphs over evil.

But out in my garden, nothing was ever that clear-cut.

For one thing, I had trouble telling the good bugs from the bad, and I wasn't sure what I would do about it if I could. To tell the difference between a tachinid fly, the good bug, and a housefly, the bad bug, I had to look for large bristles on the fly's abdomen. A ground beetle, which eats slugs, is distinguished from a darkling beetle, which eats plants, by a ridge on the head from which the ground beetle's antennae protrude. I couldn't get close enough to these bugs to see them well, and they rarely sat still long enough for me to run inside, find my book so I could look them up, and come back outside to look for their ridges or bristles.

It was probably best not to interfere in this intricate war between the bugs anyway. It was a civil war, and I was a third party, large and powerful, but unfamiliar with the history and customs of the natives. Once, I wiped out an entire cache of yellow eggs on the underside of an aphid-infested artichoke leaf, convinced that I was doing a good thing by destroying the young of the evil Mexican bean beetle. Instead, I realized later, I had taken out a nursery of ladybug eggs that would have eventually hatched into hungry, aphid-eating larvae and saved my artichokes from destruction. I felt terrible about it. For weeks afterward, I apologized to every ladybug I saw.

I decided to take on a slightly different role after that, more like the Red Cross, providing food and medical supplies, but otherwise staying out of the way. I planted yarrow and mint, chamomile and thyme, plants that offer up plenty of pollen and nectar. I scattered seeds of cosmos and goldenrod and calendula, and it all came up, blooming in a careless, mismatched sort of way, carpeting the space between the vegetable beds and the flower borders like a wildflower meadow. These flowers, the books promised me, would attract all the very best bugs, the most worthy and desirable of insects, who would stop by for a snack and enjoy the neighborhood so much that they would decide to settle down and raise a family. Peace would reign in the little village that was my backyard.

THINGS DIDN'T WORK out that way, at least not at first. The warm June weather was starting to create some serious aphid problems in my backyard. They swarmed over my half-grown tomato plants and even nestled down between the leaves of each artichoke. This made harvesting artichokes tricky: The only way I could clean them was to submerge them in a sinkful of water for a half an hour and let the bugs slowly float to the surface. Then I took them out of the sink and boiled them, and a few more bugs floated away. It was a rather gruesome task to go through for a few artichokes.

I flipped through my gardening books at night, trying to

figure out what to do. There was so much to know. Ladybugs eat aphids, but they are migratory. Like the tourists, they only come for the summer. Aphids hang around during the winter, clinging to woody stems or crevices in bark. Figuring out how these bugs relate to each other in the garden, the books told me, is the key to keeping pests in check.

I was amazed at the crop reports on the university farm's Web site explaining their attempts at pest management. "We're trying to do something about earworms in the corn," I read one time. "We've planted rows of goldenrod in the cornfield. We hope this will attract minute pirate bugs, a natural predator to the earworm larvae." Such work to get rid of some earworms! What if the goldenrod doesn't come up? What if the minute pirate bugs aren't drawn to it? What if they show up but don't find the earworm larvae until it's too late?

If I really wanted to get rid of the aphids, there was that one other option, the one that was always just lurking in the background: Pesticide. The bomb. San Lorenzo devoted an entire aisle to products that got rid of bugs, and I hadn't forgotten what a thorough job they'd done on my citrus tree. But I remembered how guilty and uneasy I felt after I sprayed that tree. I must have killed as many good bugs as bad. It seemed senseless and terrible, and I often regretted it. Dropping a malathion bomb on the garden is quick, easy, and final. All the bugs die at once, and the garden becomes strangely stark, silent, and insect free. But who wants to eat chemical-coated food? Why bother growing it myself if I'm just going to spray it with the same awful stuff the supermarket produce is sprayed with? I was sure I could find an organic solution, even if it meant I had to become intimate with the feeding habits, mating rituals, and habitats of every bug in the garden, good and bad.

Ladybugs were the most obvious organic solution to my aphid problem, and I had plenty of them already. I started looking for them on my evening tours of the garden. One night, I counted at least three pairs of ladybugs on my artichokes, all involved in the act of mating. The more I looked, the more I realized that there was more sex happening in my garden than in a San Francisco bathhouse. In fact, I felt a little embarrassed, like a child who'd wandered into her parent's bedroom on Saturday morning by mistake. I felt like I shouldn't be there. I backed away slowly, averting my eyes to give them some privacy.

I was glad the ladybugs had arrived, but I feared they were too late. The aphids were reproducing faster than the ladybugs could eat them. I thought about bringing in more from the nursery as reinforcements, but I'd heard that store-bought ladybugs tend to fly away, and besides, they might not get along with the local ladybugs who were here first. I had no idea this would be so complicated. I was running out of options.

Then one day, San Lorenzo had something different on the shelf where they usually kept the cartons of ladybugs: tall plastic bottles that looked just like juice bottles; but instead of being filled with juice, they contained sawdust and hundreds of tiny lacewing eggs. According to the directions on the package, the eggs would hatch into lacewing larvae, which would eat aphids voraciously for about three weeks. After that, they would change into "attractive egg-laying adults" and take up residence in the garden.

I was sold. I bought a bottle and took it home to release into my garden. The lacewings came with a stack of little cone-shaped paper cups, the kind they give you at the dentist's office to rinse out your mouth. I was supposed to attach the paper cups to aphid-infested plants and trees around the yard and fill them with the sawdust/lacewing egg mixture. When the eggs hatched, the larvae would crawl out of the cups and start destroying my aphid population.

I arranged the cups around the garden, affixing some of them to the tomato supports with twist ties, nestling some into tree branches, tucking a few between the leaves and the stem of my artichoke plant. I filled each one with sawdust and eggs, and sprinkled the rest directly onto the opening artichoke buds, where, I figured, they could hatch and begin eating immediately.

Scott came outside to check on my progress. "How do you know there are actually lacewing eggs in here?" he asked, rifling through the sawdust with a finger.

"Leave them alone!" I told him, pulling his hand away. "They're in there. Look closer. See those tiny green eggs?"

He peered into the cup. "Oh, I see one!" he said, looking up at me triumphantly. "It looks like an aphid."

"It is not an aphid. It is an Aphid Destroyer. Says so right here on the package."

"Well, all these cups look pretty silly out here. Couldn't they have given you something more natural-looking to use? Something that would blend in a little?"

I had to admit he was right there. The paper cones did look a little ridiculous clipped onto all my plants. I never saw a single lacewing larva, or an adult lacewing, in my garden after that. After a month or so, I went out and rounded up the paper cups, and there were still aphids on the tomato plants and the orange tree. I did notice, however, that my artichoke plant was completely free of aphids for weeks after that. Maybe the lacewings had done their work and moved on to another garden. Maybe, in the end, my aphids weren't interesting enough to make them want to stay around.

APHIDS WEREN'T MY ONLY PROBLEM. The snails were starting to become a serious threat, devouring rows of lettuce in a single evening, nibbling basil down to the ground as soon as I planted it. They seemed more difficult to control than the aphids; they were larger, more substantial, and they required a direct confrontation. Spraying them hard with the hose would not make them fly away. There was no tiny predator that would come into my yard and politely devour them. I had heard that ducks ate snails, but introducing a duck into the yard would complicate things and would surely escalate the insect war to a whole new level. LeRoy would get involved, chasing the duck around, or worse, the duck would chase LeRoy. Gray would look away with haughty disdain, but she'd show her displeasure with me by refusing to sleep on my pillow at night. It could upset the balance of the entire household.

I mentioned the problem to my mother one night. I should have known she would have some good advice. "Well," she said, "you remember that back in Texas we used bowls of beer to keep snails and slugs out of the cat food on the front porch." She reminded me that snails (like many Texans) can't resist beer and will crawl right into a bowl of it, oblivious to their rapidly dissolving relatives at the bottom of the bowl. "It's sort of a redneck approach to snail control," she said.

I did remember that. The only alternative to waking up to a bowl of cat food covered in enormous black slugs was to wake up to a bowl of stale beer filled with drowned slugs. I couldn't face the sight and smell of it early in the morning. If that was the only way to get rid of them, the snails were safe, at least for the moment.

But I enjoyed calling around for advice. I had no idea there were so many different ways to get rid of snails. Everybody had their own method. When I called Scott's Aunt Barbara, she said, "Oh, the salt shaker and flashlight method has always worked for me. Go outside at night when they've come out of hiding, and sprinkle a little salt on them. But stand back—they do foam up." This had the same drawback as the bowl of beer—I'd have to deal with their slimy, half-dissolved bodies after I killed them. I just couldn't face it. Besides, I was getting along pretty well with the neighbors these days. I didn't want to alarm Charlie and Beverly by stalking through my yard late at night in my bathrobe, with a flashlight in one hand and a salt shaker in the other.

Eventually, I decided to take the advice of my gardening books, which all recommended handpicking snails. ("Handpicking," I learned, is a gardening euphemism for systematically hunting down and killing in a quick and violent manner.) The idea was to pick them up one at a time and dispose of them somehow. A direct confrontation. No salt or beer or predators as intermediaries. It would just be woman against snail. This appealed to me.

I walked outside early in the morning and—carefully, tentatively—lifted a snail off one of my lettuce plants, grasping its shell lightly between my fingers. It came away from the plant reluctantly, and it was only after I managed to slide it along the leaf for a minute that it finally let go. I stood holding it, looking into its tiny gray face, which was rapidly retracting into its shell. Now I had to figure out what to do with it. The gardening books suggested stepping on it, but I didn't think I could stand the crunch of its shell under my foot. I also didn't want its slimy little corpse on my walkway afterward. I walked around the garden with it, nervous, uncertain. The snail was starting to get restless, too. It stuck one slimy antenna out of its shell, then another. I could feel its body moving around in the shell. What would a snail do if it was provoked? What kind of aggressive behavior was it about to unleash on me? A little bit of foam started bubbling out from under its shell. More out of fright than anything else, I tossed the snail into the street. In a few minutes, a car drove by and crushed it under a tire.

Aha! I didn't have to kill them after all! I could throw them into the road and let some unsuspecting motorist do it for me! Why hadn't the gardening books told me that in the first place?

I picked up a few more snails and tossed them into the street. Some of them looked downright nervous about it, casting their antennae about wildly, squirming around in their shells. I started talking to them as I threw them, hoping that perhaps they'd listen to reason. "Look," I muttered to a large, tough-shelled snail, "if you'd just kept off my basil, it wouldn't have to come to this."

I was starting to feel like the Spaniard in *The Princess Bride,* engaging in a little verbal banter during the duel. I decided to try his famous line, the one he waited his whole life to say to his enemy just before he killed him. I plucked one last snail from its resting place and said loudly, "My name is Inigo Montoya. You killed my basil. Prepare to die." It waved its frightened gray antennae at me one last time, and I flung it into traffic.

How to Make a Bug Love You

The single best way to attract good bugs to the garden is to plant a border of herbs and flowers designed just for them. Beneficial insects prefer plants with very small flowers, and with that in mind, I usually plant a border around my vegetable garden that includes:

- *Dill, cilantro, and parsley:* All three of these annual herbs put out sprays of small, lacy flowers. The yellow dill blossoms are particularly lovely and work well as filler in flower arrangements. They'll attract aphid-eating thrips.

- *Oregano:* Look for the highly ornamental Hopley's with its dark purple flowers, great for dried flower arrangements and hard for bees to resist.

- *Catnip and catmint:* Catnip has a more upright growing habit and pink or white flowers, while catmint, with bluish-purple flowers tends to sprawl along the ground more. It's also a little less attractive to cats, so it's more likely to survive in a garden inhabited by cats. Both attract plenty of pollinators.

- 🐝 *Tansy:* Related to the carrot. I planted one right next to an artichoke plant and never saw a single aphid, thanks to the ladybugs it attracted. Another artichoke, planted just a few feet away, was covered in the pests. Go figure.

- 🐝 *Culinary sage:* When left to bloom, it puts out stalks of small pink flowers that will be covered by bees. Good in dried arrangements. Cut it back when the blooms are spent and you may get a second round of flowers before the year ends.

- 🐝 *Feverfew:* An old-fashioned headache remedy, this plant has lacy foliage and small, white or yellow pom-pom flowers that attract all kinds of helpful bugs.

- 🐝 *Queen Anne's lace:* Considered a weed in some parts of the country, but there are cultivated varieties that put out stronger blooms and look less rangy. Airy white flowers are popular among beneficial wasps and make a good filler in floral arrangements.

- 🐝 *Yarrow:* Comes in a range of pastel colors very attractive to butterflies. I've also seen ladybugs swarm over it.

In addition, I scatter leftover seeds from the vegetable garden, like carrot and mustard, which I know will attract good bugs when they go to seed.

Houseplants

There is no use trying to grow houseplants
unless one is willing to be a nurse.

—KATHARINE WHITE,
Onward and Upward in the Garden, 1958

All the time I'd been gardening outdoors,
I'd been gardening indoors, too. Houseplants had taken up residence in every room of the
house, almost without my realizing it. I wasn't sure how
they all got here, and I was even less sure that I wanted
them to stay.

It took several months for me to admit how I felt about
them. I used to think that all gardeners had houseplants,
that gardeners were in fact so obsessed with things that
grow that they surrounded themselves with them, plunk-
ing down a ficus or a spider plant at their bedside, in the

kitchen, even in the bathroom. As if we can't be apart from our plants for a single minute.

The truth is, though, that all the time I was gardening indoors, I secretly hated houseplants. They bored me. They didn't do anything—no flowers, no fruit, nothing. They made all kinds of picky demands about water and light and, unbelievably, they even demanded to be cleaned occasionally. I didn't even dust my own bookshelves. Why would I dust my plants? If they were outside, where they belonged, they'd either get washed clean by the rain or they'd learn not to mind a little dirt.

For months I couldn't confess to anyone, not even myself, that I felt this way. And because of that, houseplants came to me the way cats always go to the people who are allergic to them.

Ivy came first. It always does. "Here," a friend said one day, "take a cutting from my ivy. Just stick it in water and it will root—but of course, you're a gardener, so it will really take off for you."

Damn, I thought. But I stuck it in a glass of water and set it on the back of the toilet where, to my disgust, it flourished.

All the other easy-to-propagate houseplants, like grape ivy and philodendron, followed in rapid succession. A spider plant sent one of its babies over my cubicle wall at work one day, and a hand belonging to my coworker appeared with a pair of scissors; she snipped it from the mother plant as if she were cutting an umbilical cord and said, "All yours!" Why I didn't just sweep it in the trash is beyond me, but instead, I dutifully stuck it into a clay pot and let it take root in a little sterile potting soil that I actually had to go out and buy especially for it.

Pretty soon I had dozens of houseplants. Don't ask me where they all came from. I think I may have even bought a few of them myself, in some attempt to broaden my horizons, to diversify my collection. I had ficus trees, rubber trees, and plants with vaguely offensive names like mother-in-law tongue and wandering Jew. Plants I didn't care a thing about. I resented watering them. I resented feeding them the watery blue solution of fertilizer. Why can't they take care of themselves? Why do I do things for them—wash their leaves, move them from room to room whenever they pout—that I don't even do for my *real* plants, the ones that live outside in the real garden?

And the bugs! It was as if they invited all their creepy friends over without asking my permission first. I found whitefly *in my house*. Aphids. Even scale. All the disgusting creatures I'd been doing battle with in my garden started finding their way inside. I didn't mind confronting them on their own turf, but I just didn't know how to handle them inside. Could I release some ladybugs into my living room? Would Scott mind if I sprayed the kitchen with insecticidal soap?

I got disgusted with the plants and their nasty pest infestations. Pretty soon, I couldn't stand to look at them. I barely watered them after a while, and I certainly never took the time to mix up any fertilizer for them. They got sicker, droopier. The bugs reproduced. A new generation set up camp.

Then one day, I wrapped a whole plant, pot and all, in a garbage bag and carried it out to the trash. It was too insect-ridden to leave out on the curb for someone to take, but I felt a twinge of guilt anyway. I half-expected the ground to open up and swallow me, or lightning to strike me down, for angering the gods of gardening. But nothing like that happened. No one seemed to notice at all, so one by one, the plants disappeared like this.

Scott didn't mind. He never liked the houseplants much, anyway. Certain plants gave him the creeps—columbine, for instance, with long spurs that reminded him of devil's horns I wasn't willing to give up growing columbine for him—I thought they were graceful, enchanting flowers. But I would happily give up spider plants, which he hated for much the same reason as he hated the columbine. "They look like some species of alien plant," he said, "that has landed here and started sending its offspring down from the ship."

A houseplant-free home was my goal, but it was hard, because they arrived almost as fast as I threw them out. My aunt brought me an ivy cutting all the way from my great-grandmother Mammy's house in Texas, and I couldn't refuse it. We also had two hardy green ficus trees that I decided to hang on to.

And then one day, I came home with an orchid, something elegant and unusual, something that takes a little skill and finesse to grow. It had pink flowers that dangled gracefully off a long stalk, and a spray of modest leaves at its base. I might not mind orchids, I thought. Even Scott was interested in them because, being a collector, he was interested in anything rare and unusual that people collect. Orchids seemed like an appropriate indoor plant for a gardener and a book collector. And sure enough, people started bringing them to me as soon as they found out I had one.

After a while, I had a little collection of them, all sitting in trays full of marbles with water in the bottom to create a damp, tropical atmosphere around them. They were intriguing plants. They bloomed, and then they went dormant, then they bloomed again. They lived in bark. They didn't like to be watered the regular way—they preferred to be taken over to the sink, one at a time, and to have the water run over their roots, the way it would happen in their native rain forests, where they lived high in the trees and waited for the afternoon rains. They were like foreign exchange students, with far more interesting customs and cuisines than the messy lumbering American teenagers I had had for houseplants before. I scurried after them, taking them to the sink for a little tropical rain, buying them special pink orchid food, changing their bark, and moving them from window to window if I thought they were getting too hot or too cold. As far as I could tell, they didn't know what had happened to all the houseplants who used to live here before them. I hoped they wouldn't find out. I was enjoying this fresh start, this second chance. I was happy to look after them, and so far, they were happy to be here.

Orchids: Houseplants Worth Having

Orchids don't deserve their reputation for being hard to care for. When British collectors first began sponsoring expeditions to collect orchids from the rain forests of South

America, they didn't understand enough about their customary growing conditions to keep them alive. Many rare and exotic orchids were made extinct as collectors fumbled around for the right growing medium, temperature, and humidity. During the Victorian era there was even a machine invented to dunk orchids into vats of water to keep them from drying out.

But today, the likes and dislikes of orchids are much better understood, and just about anybody can keep an orchid or two alive in their home. *Phalaenopsis* and *Cymbidium* are two popular varieties that do well as houseplants and don't require much special treatment.

First of all, orchids live in bark, not water. They are accustomed to growing high in the treetops of a rain forest, where they root in tree bark and take advantage of the nutrients that wash down the tree with the rain. To mimic this condition, orchids are sold in fast-draining pots full of "orchid bark," a small bark that will absorb a little water and let the rest wash away. If the plant has been in the pot a long time, the bark may have started to decompose into something that looks more like soil; if this is the case, it should be repotted.

People think of orchids growing in warm, steamy greenhouses and wonder how they can survive in an ordinary living room. Actually, you can provide enough humidity for most orchids by setting the plants into shallow trays filled with a layer of river rock, or other decorative pebbles, and pouring a little water into the tray. As the water evaporates, it adds moisture to the air right around the plant. Since orchids grow best in plastic pots, you can also find a decorative pot with no hole in the bottom that is slightly larger than the plastic pot your orchid grows in. Line the bottom of the decorative pot with pebbles, add a little water, and set the plastic pot inside it.

Orchids do need a general-purpose houseplant fertilizer in order to do well (there are also special orchid fertilizers sold, but regular houseplant food is just fine if that's what you happen to have). Two to three times a week, take your orchids over to the sink and run water over the bark. Once every week or two, use a solution of diluted fertilizer instead of plain water. After you water them, let them sit in the sink for half an hour and do it again, to ensure that the bark has absorbed enough water to sustain the roots.

Every variety of orchid has different requirements regarding light and temperature. Most like bright, indirect light and evening temperatures of fifty-five to sixty degrees. Some prefer a dry, cool season as a resting period after they're finished blooming.

Clearing a Path

A little studied negligence is becoming to a garden.

—Eleanor Perényi, Green Thoughts, 1981

Once when we were on vacation in British Columbia, Scott and I went to the Butchart Gardens, a world-famous ornamental garden. We arrived with a busload of tourists and found ourselves herded through "Fifty Acres of Floral Finery," as the brochure described it: manicured lawns, washes of bright annuals, and formal borders, all planted in perfect symmetry just that spring and waiting to be yanked out and replaced come winter. There was not a weed in sight, and not a single flower or bulb was allowed to pop up spontaneously in a neighboring bed. Anything that didn't adhere to the plan got yanked up or snipped back before the tour buses arrived in the morning.

We spent a couple of hours walking down the roped-off paths. I pretended to be interested in the rows of pansies, impatiens, and dwarf dahlias that carpeted the gardens. After all, we had traveled over three hours by bus, ferry, and taxi to reach this very popular tourist destination. Finally, though, I had to admit that the Butchart Gardens just didn't do it for me. I longed for the diversity and disarray of the wild. I didn't feel any closer to nature in this showboat garden; instead, I felt like I had spent my afternoon strolling through a very sterile, well-landscaped theme park or shopping mall. I kept expecting some staff member to rush up in a starched pin-striped shirt and sweep away any seedpods or leaves that had fallen into the path.

My garden didn't look anything like that. By July, it had become a little wild, a little unkempt. To some, it may have seemed charming and sweetly disheveled, and to others, it may have looked uncared for and neglected. If I had to choose a way of thinking about it, I would have chosen the former. Still, I worried that I had failed as a gardener in some small way. I was careless; I was impatient. I never did much in the way of planning, and it showed. The ongoing maintenance chores—pulling weeds, picking suckers off the tomato vines, and repotting the geraniums—bored me. The excitement of planting a garden from scratch was beginning to fade, and in its place I had this weedy, rambling jumble of plants to take care of.

I forgot to stake my flowers, and the sunflowers leaned slowly to the right (always the right, I was never sure why) until the stems buckled, one at a time, and the flower heads came to rest on the ground. I planted some shrubs too close together, and they competed for space like kids in the backseat, fighting over the sunniest spot and kicking each other's roots underground. After a while, they started to look a little frail and sickly from the effort. And I left some areas entirely unplanted, for reasons that weren't really clear even to me. Half the side yard, for instance, was in shade, and every time I wandered into the shady plant section of San Lorenzo to find something to plant there, I got bored and distracted and wandered back to the sun-loving flowers. Eventually I gave up and let the blackberries take over in the shade, a silly choice since without sun, they didn't stand a chance of producing a single berry.

I worked on convincing myself that this disarray in the flower beds was actually a good thing. I had begun to collect books on cottage gardening, and I was pretty sure that was what I had. A mix of tall, flowering annuals and perennials, all jumbled together, tended to with only the lightest touch. A flower garden should be more than a cookie-cutter de-sign, the books told me, more than a six-inch-high carpet of color that gets fertilized and pampered into bloom for a short, frantic season. A little wilderness is essential in a flower garden. There should be overgrown shrubs, dried seed pods, and dormant perennials that are allowed to stay green and rest. Try to control it too much, and it will never get where it needs to go. Let it tend toward wilderness whenever it can, advised the books. If it looked disheveled, well, maybe it was meant to be that way.

This kind of advice appealed to me. Let it go. Don't control it too much. The ladybugs and the butterflies didn't seem to mind, so why should I? Over time, I started to enjoy this laid-back approach to the flower beds. I developed a very Santa Cruz, New Age outlook on the whole thing. I was *in tune* with the garden. I would let *it* tell *me* what to do.

I had a chance to put this approach to the test one night when I got home from work about an hour before Scott and I were going to leave for a night in San Francisco. The tourists had finally gotten to be too much for us; we were headed to a high-rise hotel where we could be tourists ourselves for a couple of days and enjoy the pleasures of the big city, like a play in the theater district and a restaurant where something more formal than sandals was required. It only took a few minutes to get ready for our trip: pack a small bag, leave some food out for the cats, wash whatever dishes were left in the sink. I hustled around the house, getting ready to go and keeping an eye on the evening news. I was not thinking about the garden, until I dropped my overnight bag by the door and caught sight of four six-packs of cosmos seedlings sitting on the porch, already tall and rootbound. I had bought them at the nursery the week before and forgotten to plant them. If I left them outside all weekend, they would dry out and wilt in the summer heat. I knew I had to get them in the ground right away, before we left for the city.

There were only about fifteen minutes left before Scott was to get home and we had to leave. I stepped outside with the seedlings in my hand and stopped short. Where was I going to plant these things? For once, the flower beds looked crowded, too full to accept even a few more seedlings. I hadn't bought them because I had any particular place in mind for them; I had intended to just tuck them in wherever I found a spot.

I was completely stumped. I wasn't sure why at first. I could jam a row of lettuce into the ground in ten minutes flat if I was in a hurry. Mark a line in the dirt with a shovel, make a row of holes, drop the seedlings in. It is a mechanical process requiring no particular thought or attention, and if the soil is prepared and an empty row is waiting, it takes me no time at all to plant it. But this was different.

These Picotee cosmos didn't belong in a straight row in the kitchen garden. They were wild-looking, free-ranging flowers that would grow to six feet tall and fill the air with their sunny petals and lacy foliage. I thought back to the advice in my cottage garden books about giving flowers free reign. I knew I couldn't tell them where to go. They would have to tell me where to plant them.

I turned the six-pack upside down and let one seedling fall into my hand. I shook the dirt off the root ball and walked around the garden slowly, looking for the perfect spot for it. Just then, I heard a voice: *Here, next to the patio,* the seedling whispered. *And get two or three more to plant around me.*

I should say right now that the plants didn't speak to me directly. There was no *actual* voice giving me orders. It was more of an instinct, a kind of quiver in my gut that got stronger as I got closer to the right place. Like a divining rod. I have come to believe that most gardeners have one of these, although we don't talk about them and the topic isn't covered in any gardening book that I've ever seen. This instinctual feeling about where to plant, this sort of gardening divination, stays silent during the planning process, the afternoons spent indoors with graph paper and colored pencils. It sits quietly by while I study up on light and water requirements, companion planting, and soil types. It allows elaborate studies of height and color to go on uninterrupted. But when I was standing in the garden with a seedling in my hand, it cleared its throat and spoke up. *Don't plant us all in the corner like that,* it said. *Scatter a few around up front. Put me over there in the herb garden.* I listened to this little voice and I did what it told me. What else could I do? After all, these plants should have some say about where they get to live. They were the ones who had to survive out here, not me.

My great-grandmother Mammy would not have been surprised to hear that my seedlings were talking to me. She was on intimate terms with the inhabitants of her own garden, knowing at once who was happy where he was and who felt lonely tucked away in the back. "Stand up straight," she once said to a pansy on her front porch, brushing the blossom as if she were chucking it under the chin. "You're just like your brothers, always slouching."

My mother would understand also. She carried on her own intimate relationships with her houseplants, nudging and coercing them into thriving in our sunny living room, murmuring gratefully to them when they cooperated. She once took my brother and me to New Mexico, where we drove through the mountains with her friend Linden. He glanced in his rearview mirror just in time to catch me waving to a field of wildflowers. "Uh-oh," he said, shaking his head. "She's signaling to the flowers. She's just like her mom."

Now, standing in the garden, I knew Scott would be home any minute. I only had a few minutes left, but this work couldn't be rushed. Each flower wanted to be planted in its own spot. I found myself strolling to the front porch to drop one in a planter, and back to the vegetable garden to plant the last one behind the tomatoes, where, it told me, it would be the lone pink flower in a row of bright yellow sunflowers.

So THE FLOWERS AND I got along as best we could. I followed their instructions, mostly. I tried to pull weeds and pick off dead seedpods, but other than that, I resisted any temptation to tidy up, to organize, to impose a sense of order. It looked good—a little unruly, but good.

The vegetable garden was another matter entirely. It suffered from the same lack of structure, only more so, somehow. It started out well enough—one large square of cleared earth, with vegetable seedlings planted in straight lines. Then, when I started planting from seed, I found that the seeds had a tendency to wander, popping up a couple of rows over, and pretty soon the rows blurred together and I simply had one large, mismatched patch. It wasn't even square anymore. As I added rows, they seemed to come out at an angle, until I had a large trapezoid that sat awkwardly in the space between Charlie's fence and the citrus trees.

I was embarrassed about the way my vegetable garden looked—like someone took a real garden, the kind with color schemes and geometric planting patterns, and dumped it into my backyard from a helicopter. I worried over the misshapen mounds planted with scraggly seedlings, the weedy, uneven borders around the bed. It looked unreliable, unloved. How could anyone want to eat something that grew out of a mess like this?

I turned back to my cottage garden books. They all had a section on potagers, kitchen gardens named after the French word *potage,* a thick vegetable soup flavored with strong herbs. A potager is, by definition, a human creation, the books told me. Its success or failure depends on the gardener's skills and abilities. The vegetables grown there are often not wild or native to any place; they are products of centuries' worth of careful cultivation and breeding, and they require plenty of care and attention. A kitchen garden should be tidy and orderly, a sign that it has been well planned and cared for. It should look like a sane and rational person is tending it. There should be a boundary around it, and a path through it. This is a good balance in a garden, the books reassured me, the neat rows of vegetables bordered by the wild, riotous flower beds.

The books had a point. A little organization would go a long way. I decided it was time to make some changes. The vegetable garden was too small, anyway; I had plans for a big expansion next year. I could lay it out now, at the height of summer—just dig the beds and lay a path. The vegetables I'd already planted could stay right where they were; I'd work around them. They'd have plenty of room to sprawl, and in the spring, I could start again with two or three times as many vegetables.

But first I had to find a good design. As it turned out, there were an amazing number of different ways to lay out a rectangular vegetable garden. You could plant straight rows, either vertically or horizontally. I rejected that idea right away, given my history with keeping the rows straight. Besides, I wanted something a little more interesting, a little more geometrical, as a way of proving that I could in fact plan a neat, well organized garden.

Small square beds, laid out in a checkerboard pattern, were another obvious choice. The size of each bed made them easy to handle; you could lean across them to work, and inside each square you could plant your vegetables in short rows or diamond patterns or, in the case of larger plants like squash or artichokes, you could put one plant in a mound in the center, with a row of edible flowers or herbs around the edge. Square beds also had the advantage of making crop rotation easy, and this was important in a vegetable garden according to the gardening books piling up on my nightstand. Plants like tomatoes should not be planted in the same place twice or diseases would build up in the soil; each bed needed a long resting period between different types of crops. If you planted tomatoes or peppers one year, you might plant beans there the next year, and corn or squash the year after. The neat, compact grid would allow for this annual shuffling of vegetables—get the order right in the first year, then bump everything over by one square each year. But this seemed too regimented to me, too military. The idea of all those little squares made me nervous. What if I forgot which way I'd been rotating them and moved them all back a square to the exact same spot they'd been the year before?

The design possibilities only got more elaborate from there. Since medieval times, the French have been planting vegetables in mazes of triangles and diamonds and half-circles called *parterres*. The small, oddly shaped beds were easier to weed and allowed for denser, more efficient planting than a traditional square bed. The beds were bordered by a clipped hedge of boxwood or lavender, and herringbone brick paths ran through them. These designs were originally popular for ornamental shrubs and flowers, but in 1914, faced with the realities of a country at war, the gardeners at the Château de Villandry in France planted their ornamental parterre with vegetables. Lowly cabbages and pumpkins were elevated to an art form in the chateau's elegant garden, where purple cabbages were paired with blue leeks for the color contrast, summer squash grew agreeably within the bounds of a box hedge, and scarlet runner beans scrambled up the baroque iron lattices. With Villandry as a role model, the notion of the vegetable garden as a highly decorative showplace became more popular.

Not surprisingly, these ornamental gardens present a few practical problems. When a design is built around the precise placement of the plants — say, a bed of alternating red and green lettuce, or a diamond-shaped cabbage patch bordered by curly parsley — harvesting becomes extremely disruptive. Even the hungriest gardener would be hard put to pull up a row of beets for dinner if it meant destroying the garden's carefully constructed design. Some people get around this problem by harvesting every other vegetable, so that the structure is maintained and thinned out evenly. But I wonder: What happens if the cabbages come to maturity out of order, and the next one due for picking is not yet ripe, while all the others, the ones that must remain behind to keep order in the bed, are actually begging to come out of the ground?

One way around this is to have a "working bed" somewhere out of sight, crammed full of seedlings that are ready to go in the ground whenever a mature vegetable is harvested. If you want an onion, you can have it, but there must be a seedling in the back bed to take its place. It would not take me long to figure out a way around this chore of replacing every vegetable I picked: I would harvest my vegetables directly from the working bed, and leave the ornamental bed untouched, like a formal parlor that never gets used.

As silly as these showboat gardens sounded, I couldn't resist searching through some design books for ideas. Surely there was something I could adapt to my little garden. Arches and tunnels, for instance, get used a lot in decorative gardens to add some architectural interest. I could make a bamboo archway entrance to my garden and let the pole beans climb up it. Or I could build the design around a central, striking plant, like a giant artichoke or a dwarf fruit tree. Anything seemed possible, as I leafed through the glossy pages. I was particularly entranced with one large, incredibly intricate kitchen garden with a formal knot herb garden at one end. I could do that, I thought, just on a smaller scale. Then I turned the page and realized I'd been looking at a picture of Versailles.

Maybe not. I went out to look at the site of my future vegetable bed and think it over. It had seemed so large before, when I first decided to clear it and devote the whole space to vegetables, but as I looked at the lavish French estate gardens, my own plot of land seemed small, ridiculously small. A parterre would be out of place in my Santa Cruz garden, overdressed.

Finally, I settled on a simple but elegant design: four triangles that met in the center, created by making one large X-shaped path. It was a good design, easy enough for me to maintain, but interesting enough to look like I'd given some thought to it. Each bed would be large enough to hold several different vegetables, and there would be plenty of room for permanent crops like artichokes and asparagus.

Now I had to decide how to make the paths. I had rejected brick and stone as too formal, and too permanent for a rent house. One book recommended grass paths, but I didn't have the patience to wait for a crop of grass to grow, and besides, I didn't want to have to water it. I just wanted something simple and cheap that would keep the weeds down and look tidy. Rice straw seemed like an obvious choice, and I could buy it at a feed store in town. It would give the garden an agricultural feel, as if I'd just been tending to the horses and decided to use an extra straw bale to mulch the crops. It would look orderly and professional. People would see my garden, with its neat rows of vegetables and straw-lined paths, and think, "Now this is the work of a serious gardener!"

A bale of rice straw costs about five bucks, and it just fit into the trunk of my car. I brought it home from the feed store and threw it down on my newly created paths, using less than half the bale. When I was finished, Scott came outside and stood with his arm around me, admiring all the changes in the garden. "It looks just like a miniature organic farm," he said, and I stood with him and looked it over. The clean yellow straw marking the borders of each bed made all the difference. Just as I had let my flower gardens go a little wild, I had managed to bring a little more order to my vegetable beds. They struck a nice balance at opposite ends of the backyard, with the fruit trees between them. I hauled the rest of the straw bale into the garage, where it gave off a sweet hay smell that reminded me of barns. Scott was right—I had a backyard farm of my own, with its summer vegetables starting to ripen, a shed stocked with straw and shovels and rakes, and in between, in the flower beds, a little wilderness, just creeping in around the edges.

The Ultimate Design

I haven't given up on the idea of having a formal French parterre someday. It feels a little disloyal to dream about an exotic and glamorous new garden when I am out working in my first small garden by the sea. *How could you?* I can hear the ground protesting. *After all we've been through together? I'm not enough for you anymore?*

So I keep my thoughts to myself and hope the garden can't read minds. I dream of designs I might employ someday: Japanese family crests, Celtic knots, patchwork quilts, and stained-glass windows—anything intricate and geometric that could serve as a planting scheme. I'll pick crazy color combinations of vegetables and flowers for each bed, like white chard and dusty miller, red lettuce and orange marigold, and purple cabbage with blue lobelia. Tall plants like pole beans and tomatoes will stand in islands in the center, drawing the eye upward, where it will meet the sunflowers and the hollyhocks around the edges.

Here are a few design tips I've picked up along the way:

🐚 With string and stakes, map out the design in the garden. The trick is to use a ruler and mark the string carefully to get the exact spacing of every plant right (no listening to the frivolous whims of a cosmos in this planting scheme!).

❦ Use edible flowers and annual herbs to create a visual frame around each bed. Pink chives, Johnny jump-ups, and curly parsley are great choices.

❦ Any garden has a tendency to get overgrown and wild looking. Pick a formal material for your paths, to provide some extra structure. A herringbone brick pattern, or a simple walk made from square concrete pavers, will help to emphasize the design.

❦ Give some height to the garden with trellises, dwarf fruit trees, or stands of tall plants like corn. Space these elements equally to lend an additional air of formality.

❦ Think carefully about your plants' maturation times so everything doesn't come ripe at once and throw your design off. Red lettuce and corn, for instance, are a good combination because the lettuce will be ready to pick long before the corn is mature. In fact, you could get a crop of spring lettuce out of the ground and replace it with heat-loving purple basil while the corn is still growing.

First Visitor

My garden has been visited by a High Official Person. President Grant was here just before the Fourth. . . . I thought of putting up over my gate, "Welcome to the Nation's Gardener," but I hate nonsense, and didn't do it. I, however, hoed diligently on Saturday: what weeds I couldn't remove I buried, so that everything would look all right. The borders of my drive were trimmed with scissors; and everything that could offend the Eye of the Great was hustled out of the way.

—Charles Dudley Warner,
My Summer in a Garden, 1870

So far, the garden hadn't had any visitors to speak of. My parents came into town once or twice and followed me around the yard, admiring my work. They looked enthusiastically at the bright blooming sunflowers; they peered into the worm bin with raised eyebrows. I tried to make sure I had something to offer them when they came: a bouquet of flowers, a plate of grilled squash. I laid these treasures in front of them with pride, and in return, they dished out praise and compliments.

But they were *family*. They'd be thrilled with anything I did. It wasn't until my friend Annette called from Albuquerque to say that she was coming to visit that I realized what an intensely personal accomplishment a garden could be, how easily it could fail to live up to someone's expectations, how crushed I would be if it fell short.

I almost managed to talk her out of it at first. "Where would you like to go while you're here?" I asked Annette when she called. "What about the wine country? I could take you up to Sonoma."

"Well, that'd be fun," she said. "But what I really want to do is see where you live. Mostly, I want to see this garden I've heard so much about."

She wanted to come all the way across the country to see my garden? Perhaps I'd bragged a little too much in my letters to her. I'd told her about the herbs and vegetables I'd planted, and all the varieties of flowers, listing each one individually: "Basil, oregano, thyme, and rosemary. Poppy, calendula, sweet pea, sunflowers." It probably sounded more impressive on paper than it really was. Perhaps this was my fault. Had I embellished just a little, for lack of anything else to brag about? I wasn't sure. Maybe I had.

After I got off the phone with her, I wandered outside to work in the garden, pulling weeds mostly, and I tried to see it through someone else's eyes as I worked. I had wanted to make it pretty for the tourists, but suddenly there was one tourist whose opinion would matter more than all the rest of them combined. As I stood there thinking about it, I caught a reflection of myself in the laundry room window, a faint image of me in my garden. We were not a pretty sight. I was wearing old sweatpants and a T-shirt with ground-in manure stains. I had on a very unflattering Texas Longhorns ball cap to protect my face from the sun. Dirt was caked under my fingernails, and my gardening shoes had filled with enough compost to fertilize half the yard. For no particular reason, I was carrying around a rather brutal pair of half-rusted pruning shears. I was, in short, a mess. But it wasn't *my* appearance that worried me most. It was the garden's.

As I stood there, picking the dirt out of my ears and adjusting my hat, I mulled over my surroundings with the eye of a teenage girl who had just caught sight of her reflection in the locker room mirror. My alyssum was growing old and scraggly. I should rip it out by the roots,

I thought. The lettuce was covered in embarrassing spots. The compost heap was starting to smell funny again, and my tomatoes were pathetically small—much smaller than everyone else's.

Preparing for Annette's visit forced me to look critically at my garden, to see it for what it was, not what I wanted it to be. For instance, there was this empty spot near the front steps where, inexplicably, everything I ever planted had died. I had given up months before, after I brought in new soil, planted everything from fussy little ornamentals to easy, carefree daisies, dropped in wildflower seed, even tried an invasive ground cover that the nursery staff actually tried to talk me out of buying because, they said, it would take over. Nothing lived in that spot for more than a few weeks, and I never figured out why. After a while, I just started filling in the space mentally with whatever I imagined I'd like to see there: a blood red penstemon one week, an airy love-in-a-mist the next. My garden, I realized, was full of imaginary corrections, mirages, plants that I saw not as they were, but as I imagined them, in another year or two, when the garden would be mature and perfect. What did this place look like, really? I knew it so well that I couldn't see it anymore.

I had such hopes for the garden when we moved in. I imagined it in soft focus, misty and vague, a dream garden to match the dream house in which we lived. I paged through the garden magazines and pieced together an imaginary garden from the pictures I found there. Cucumbers climbing up a handmade trellis. Window boxes overflowing with waterfalls of blue lobelia. An entire garden devoted just to night-blooming flowers, with a wrought-iron bench in the center where Scott and I would sit together under the stars. This garden already existed in my imagination, and in time, I was sure, the reality would catch up. The problem was, it hadn't yet.

I COULDN'T IMPRESS ANNETTE with my imaginary garden; I would have to do something about the real one. Maybe I could add a few more plants and try to perk the place up. I drove over to San Lorenzo to see what I could find. I only had a couple of weeks until her visit, so whatever I bought would need to be already full-grown and blooming, ready to stand up tall in my garden and be impressive. This narrowed down my choices. Anything on the sale table, the half-wilted plants with enormous potential but not much shelf life, was out of the question. The twelve-inch-tall perennials that would grow into gorgeous, four-foot blooming shrubs in a year's time would do me no good. No, I needed something that could go into the ground instantly and look great.

Instant. That was the key word. As I walked around San Lorenzo, I kept returning to the "Instant Color" section, the rows and rows of blooming annuals that I had always ignored. I had decided long ago that I was not an "Instant Gardener." But this time, I found myself helplessly drawn toward the pansies and the marigolds—the bright reliable bloomers, the summer annuals that keep every garden center across the country in business, two dollars at a time. I had never wanted them before, but now I had the problem that they were designed to solve. I had empty space, a need for blooming color, and they would step in and do the job on a moment's notice. I looked around to make sure I was safely out of sight of the organic vegetable gardeners in the back. I didn't want them to see me loading my cart with ordinary old pansies or, worse, petunias.

Because of course, that's exactly what I did. In fact, I went a little crazy, filling up my cart with colorful annuals. They were like gardening candy, hard to resist once I got started. I bought impatiens and violas, blooming ground covers, and—I am most ashamed of this—a dozen or so flowering, one-gallon annuals like pincushion flowers and cosmos. Never in a million years did I think I'd stoop low enough to pay five dollars for something that grows so easily from seed, something that is practically a weed. I felt a little embarrassed about it. But they looked good, maybe too good for something that was supposed to have grown up in my garden. I worried that I'd given in to the gardening equivalent of a padded bra—not really mine, but for just a few dollars, I could claim they were, and no one would know the difference.

When I got home, I put my plants in the ground quickly, scarcely bothering to prepare the earth or even think about where they might grow best. I seemed to be reverting to my old habits. I needed results, and I needed them quickly. I wasn't very concerned about the long term. They could all shrivel up and die, as far as I cared, right after Annette's visit was over. They were stand-ins, temporary workers. They'd do their job and then I'd let them go.

The annuals took their place among my other plants, which all looked a little drab in comparison. I went inside and rooted around until I found an old bottle of that awful synthetic blue fertilizer I used to feed my houseplants. Would the garden mind if I gave it a few shots of non-organic food? I didn't think it could hurt anything, but I felt a little guilty as I sprayed it on, wondering if I was a bad mother for feeding my garden junk food after I had worked so hard to raise it on a healthy, well-balanced diet.

The garden didn't look any better. The pansies and the petunias looked stupid, false, out of place. They made my tender young garden look like it was wearing too much makeup. I wasn't at all sure that my hasty improvements had done any good at all. What was I thinking, planting ridiculous little pansies and sprinkling chemical fertilizers on them? Had I lost my mind?

Why was it so important that my garden look perfect, like a magazine garden, like someone's fantasy garden? I guess I still found it hard to believe that someone would fly all the way across the country, and given the choice between San Francisco, the wine country, and my garden, would choose to come visit my ragged patch by the sea.

THE STAGE WAS SET for Annette's arrival. The garden and I were on uneasy terms; it went right on being its natural self, but I kept giving in to the urge to touch it up, adding a few more pansies, squirting a little more of the blue stuff around. On the morning of her arrival, I rushed around the garden pulling weeds, yanking dead flowers off their stalks, and whispering to the plants as if they were the Von Trapp children getting ready to meet their new stepmother.

As I drove up the coast to meet Annette, I realized that I wasn't sure if I would even recognize her, or she me. We had known each other since junior high, but we hadn't seen one another since college seven years before. She'd gone on to get a Ph.D. in psychology; I'd gone on to — well, to plant a garden that I was barely on speaking terms with anymore. All this worrying about the garden had distracted me from the significance of reuniting with an old friend from the past, of seeing my life reflected in her eyes, this person who had known me when I was young and dreamy and full of plans I had no intention of ever carrying out. What would she remember about the way I'd said my life would be when I grew up? And how, in her eyes, would it measure up?

I'd wanted to be a poet, and I had only a few credits in some obscure literary magazines to show for that. I'd wanted to live on a boat, oddly, and I'd come surprisingly close by finding a house so near the water. I'd wanted to be a veterinarian, and instead I had an ancient cat who let me play at being a nurse to her in her feeble years. Had I ever said anything about wanting to be a gardener? I didn't think so. And what about Scott? At least I'd outdone myself there. He was smarter, and funnier, and much more steadfast and loyal than anyone Annette and I could have conjured up out of our limited experience with the boys at our high school in Texas. I knew that, at the very least, she'd be pleased I'd settled down well.

I met her at the hotel in San Francisco where she'd been staying for a conference. When she got off the elevator, I realized I shouldn't have worried about our not recognizing each other. After nine years, she looked exactly the same: the same bright blue eyes, the same shiny blond hair, and not a wrinkle to show for the last decade. "You haven't changed!" she said, rushing over to me. "You look exactly the same!" I didn't bother to argue, although I was sure I hadn't aged as well as she had. Instead, I picked up one of her suitcases and we headed through the lobby to my car.

"Are you really a *doctor* now?" I asked her in mock disbelief. I have always been impressed with labels.

"Well, I guess," she said, groaning. "But try telling that to my patients. I look like their granddaughter. Can you *imagine?*"

And just like that, our old conversation resumed where it had left off when we were eighteen, almost as if no time had passed at all. We had decided to go up to the wine country, after all, to taste champagne, and to drive down to Santa Cruz in the afternoon. On the way up to Sonoma County, she filled me in on the details of her wedding the previous year and her new internship at the veteran's hospital.

"God, Annette, that all sounds so . . . substantial," I said after a while.

"Substantial? What do you mean?"

"I don't know . . . so grown up, I guess. Look at you . . .

look at you and Chris. Both licensed psychologists before the age of thirty. . . ."

She interrupted. "Oh please. What about you? Great house on the beach, gorgeous garden . . ."

"Well . . . we'll see about that."

We got to Korbel around eleven and tasted every champagne they had, then wandered through their gardens, a little light-headed. Uh-oh, I thought. Bad idea to come to Korbel's garden before we go to mine. I felt like I'd stepped right into one of the magazine gardens I'd been trying to emulate. Everything about it was perfect. When a clematis climbed up an antique rosebush, it did so perfectly, blooming at every spot on the bush where there wasn't already a rosebud, as if they'd planned it that way. There was not a weed in sight. I could not find a single leaf—not one—that showed signs of having been nibbled by a snail. I walked through the garden enviously, even a little angrily. Oh, *sure,* I thought. Plant all your hanging baskets with red, white, and blue lobelia for the Fourth of July. Thirty feet of sweet peas in the back? Why not? After all, they've got a staff of gardeners and a full-time horticulturist — what else are they gonna do?

I tried to keep my bitterness to myself. I played the part of the wise garden expert, pointing out plants to Annette as we walked: Foxglove. Clematis. Rhododendron.

After a while, she asked, "Does your garden look like this?"

"Uh . . ." The champagne was making it hard to think. I was having trouble coming up with a snappy answer. "Well, no. It's . . . you know . . . smaller." Then, to distract her, I added, "Look at that entire wall covered in pink jasmine. I can smell it from here."

"When did you learn the names of all these plants?" she asked. "How do you know all this? I don't remember your being interested in plants in high school. Where did all this come from?"

I looked at her for a minute, puzzled, my head tilted to one side. I couldn't remember, either. It surprised me, too, suddenly to realize how much I'd learned. "I don't know, really. It's just one of the things that happened over the years."

"You didn't take a class? You didn't study?"

"No, it all just sort of . . . fell into place." We sat in silence for a long time, perched on a fence outside Korbel's garden, the green and gold vineyards stretching out to the horizon.

AFTER WE FINISHED AT THE WINERY, we drove back to Santa Cruz, rushing so that we could be on the beach by sunset. During the long drive, I had almost forgotten to be nervous about my garden, but I remembered as we pulled up in front of my house. There it was, unchanged from this morning, disappointingly familiar. I guess I had half-hoped that it would double in size while I was gone, that new flowers would spring from the ground and surprise us both.

Annette followed me up the stairs and walked along the perennial border alongside the house. I was expecting one of those kind remarks like, "Looks like you've done a lot of work here," or "I bet this'll really be something in a couple of years," but instead she exclaimed, without hesitation, "Oooh! It looks just like Korbel's garden!"

Even after all the time I had spent trying to push my garden into bloom, to make it grand and impressive, I had never expected her to say *that*. "You've become a better liar over the years," I told her, but secretly I was pleased. I followed her around, listening to her croon and sigh over my flowers, my vegetables, my new straw paths. I mumbled that I only wished she could have come just a month or two later, when everything would be in bloom, when all the vegetables would be ripe. Peak time in my garden, I told her, was only a month away. To myself, I thought, peak time was *always* a month away.

All my anxiety about showing off my garden seemed a little silly, a little pathetic, as I stood with her and looked around. What was I thinking? Some part of me actually believed that I could single-handedly transform my small coastal garden into one of those luxurious estates in the gardening books—and just in time for a visit from an old friend who knew me too well to expect perfection from me.

Standing in my garden with her, self-consciously snapping withered daisy blossoms off their stalks, I knew what I did have: a garden with soul. What's fun about an immaculate garden, anyway? I'd probably start to feel like I had to wipe my feet before I went outside. No, I had grown to love my garden for its character, for its failures as well as its triumphs. I had wanted a strong, wild garden, a place where I could work, and sweat, and get dirty, and that's exactly what I got. It was a *real* garden, flawed and temperamental, but it was mine all the same.

After a few minutes, Scott came outside to introduce himself. He had LeRoy draped around his neck like a stole, and they both looked a little rumpled, as if they'd just woken up from a nap, which, it turned out, they had. Gray trotted along behind them and sniffed Annette carefully. "Remember her?" I asked Gray, bending down to scratch the top of her head, and she sat looking up at both of us as if indeed she did.

Scott was the perfect tour guide for my garden. He could point out all the highlights while I stood around, sheepish, tongue-tied. "Have you met the worms yet?" Scott asked her.

"Uh . . . no, I don't think so. But I have a feeling I'm about to."

"Oh, you have to meet the worms," Scott said enthusiastically. "They're Amy's favorite pets—next to Gray, of course," and he nodded at Gray, who had jumped up on the back porch and was squinting at us in the fading sunlight.

I pulled the lid off the composter. All the worms were buried under a layer of newspaper; I pushed it aside with a hand shovel and turned over hundreds of fat red worms, all squirming to get out of the daylight. "See?" I said to Annette. "They eat all our kitchen scraps, then they leave *this* behind." Dramatically, I lifted a couple of trays off the composter and showed her the dark black earthworm castings underneath.

"I should have known you'd raise worms," she said to me. Then, turning to Scott, "Did you know that in ninth grade she refused to dissect a worm? And of course I was her lab partner, so I got stuck doing all the dissections after that."

"Well, I knew you wanted to be a doctor," I said, "so I figured it would be good training for you. Why would a writer need to know how to dissect a worm?"

"I'm not *that* kind of doctor," she said, laughing. "But

I'm sure it was good training for *something*. I'm just not sure *what*."

I would have liked to have stayed out there a little longer, telling her the story of the worms or the snails or all the good food we'd been harvesting from the garden. But the sun was going to set soon, and we had to rush down to the beach and find a place for our picnic before the tourists got all the best spots. We got there just in time to claim the last cement fire pit, and Scott and I built a fire while Annette walked up and down the shore, staring at the ocean and picking up driftwood. We sprawled in front of the fire, watching the sky grow dark and the stars come out, drinking the champagne we'd bought at Korbel. After we ate, we toasted marshmallows over the fire and spread them onto some ridiculously expensive cookies I'd bought for the occasion.

Annette looked around in wonder. "I have to say, when we were back in high school, I never would have guessed that you'd end up in a place like this."

"Yeah . . . it's weird how things work out," I said, pouring myself another glass of champagne. "It's not a bad life. And you do realize that Scott and I eat dinner on the beach like this every night."

"Oh, you do *not*," she said. She looked around at the beach, at the Boardwalk with its twinkling lights, and added, "But how do you remember to go to work every day? This is like a permanent vacation."

I laughed. "Is that really how my life looks?" I asked, and tried to picture it through her eyes—my romantic, beach-cottage-at-the-seashore life. "Why doesn't it look that way to me most of the time?"

"I dunno. Different perspective, I guess."

"I guess." I stretched out on the sand and looked up at the infinite black sky that dipped down to meet the ocean, where the horizon was dark and exquisite and unknowable. The three of us sat in silence looking up at the stars. Occasionally, one of them turned out to be a plane waiting to land in San Jose, and we watched it approach, low and silent, flying in from far out at sea and circling high above us, its lights blinking red and white, hovering just below the stars and waiting for clearance to land.

Garden Sandwich for Annette

Picnics at the beach can be complicated. There is wind and sand to contend with, and while one hand is occupied with eating, the other is usually busy with some other chore, like swatting away a curious dog, anchoring down the paper plates, or trying to find a place to set down a wineglass among the shifting sands. So when I take friends to the beach for dinner, I try to make food that's easy to handle. Here's a flattened sandwich that I invented just for Annette, designed to use plenty of my fresh produce without falling apart at the beach. Who can resist one last chance to show off?

 1 loaf wide French baguette

 5–7 leaves lettuce (from the garden)

 1 large sliced tomato

 1 thinly sliced purple onion

 10–15 basil leaves

 ½ pound Feta or fresh mozzarella cheese

 2 tablespoons prepared olive tapenade from a gourmet
  store, or a mixture of chopped olives

 Any vegetable that's abundant in the garden and suitable
  for grilling (eggplant, peppers, or zucchini, for instance)

 1 tablespoon Dijon mustard

 2 tablespoons olive oil

 1 tablespoon red wine vinegar

 Yield: 2 sandwiches

Brush the thinly sliced eggplant, peppers, or squash with olive oil. In a nonstick pan or outdoors on the grill, cook just long enough to sear each side.

Cut the basil into ribbons by rolling several leaves together and slicing into thin strips.

Slice the baguette lengthwise; spread one side with the olive tapenade and the other with Dijon mustard. Stack the grilled vegetables, tomatoes, onions, lettuce, and cheese onto one half of the bread.

Sprinkle with shredded basil, drizzle with olive oil and red wine vinegar, and place the other half of the bread on top of the sandwich.

Wrap well in waxed paper and set a wooden cutting board, a serving platter, or other heavy object (a brick or a cookbook works just fine) on top of the sandwich to flatten it. Let it sit for at least an hour, slice it while it is still wrapped in waxed paper, and wrap each slice individually before heading down to the beach.

Tomatoes

Well I do remember the first tomato I ever saw. I was ten years old, and was running down one of those old-fashioned lanes, on either side of which was the high rail fence, then so familiar to all Ohio people. Its rosy cheeks lighted up one of those fence-corners, and arrested my youthful attention.

—A. W. Livingston, Livingston and the Tomato, 1893

O f all the vegetables I grew my first year, tomatoes turned out to be the most complicated. There was so much to know, and so much that could go wrong. Tomatoes suffer from all kinds of nasty diseases for which there are really no cures, organic or otherwise. Diseases are everywhere, it seems—they spring from the soil, they blow in on the wind, and they spread from plant to plant. There is not much you can do about them. Keeping the plants spaced a few feet apart helps. Watering with drip irrigation keeps the leaves dry, and that helps, too. There are copper soaps you can spray on the leaves and microbial fungicides you can mix into the soil, but mostly, it seems, you have to stand by and watch, wincing at the first sign of a yellowed leaf or a lesion on the fruit.

"Destroy all infected plants," the gardening books advised heartlessly. This was poor advice for a first-time gardener. How could I destroy my tomato plants, after all the care I'd lavished upon them? I had built up the soil with compost and manure, and I had dutifully purchased every organic tomato product on the market, all the powders and sprays and even the red plastic mulch that was supposed to reflect up just the right spectrum of UV light for proper fruit growth. I'd spent so much on tomato-related products that I probably could have had the very finest tomatoes shipped to me directly from Italy and saved money.

So of course I didn't rip out my tomatoes the first time I saw a spot or a little leaf curl. I stuck with them, nursing them along with my crude and ineffectual remedies, feeling like a Civil War doctor who has nothing but snake oil and dirty bandages to offer the wounded. Some tomatoes fared better than others under my inexpert care. Mammy's Holland tomatoes and the cherry tomatoes both flourished, growing tall and sturdy, putting out loads of tiny green fruit. The Brandywines, with their enormous potato-shaped leaves, got wilty and spotty occasionally but seemed to put out plenty of new green leaves to replace the ones near the bottom that died away. The others were usually scraggly and anemic, with more leaves turning brown every day, but they kept producing fruit, so I encouraged them.

I was interested in heirloom tomatoes, with their funny names and colorful histories. While there is some argument over exactly what is meant by the term *heirloom,* it generally seems to mean any tomato whose seeds date back to before 1940. Heirloom tomatoes are grown for their extraordinary taste, but it was their unusual names that drew me in at first. Brandywine sounded heavenly, divine, and in fact, they were—I'd bought some from the farmers market and tasted them while mine were still small and green. I understood at once why they were considered the tomato lover's tomato—they had that full, ripe, height-of-summer tomato taste that tomato lovers dream of all winter long.

One of my favorite tomato names was Black from Tula. The seed catalog described it as "dark, purply brown with green shoulders" with a "perfect acid-sugar balance and wonderful, fine texture." But I didn't care about any of that. I just wanted to be able to say the name when people asked me what tomatoes I was growing. Black from Tula could be an obscure Miles Davis record, a spy novel set in a dark Russian bar, or a kind of forbidden caviar served with ice cold vodka. I might not have been hip and avant-garde enough to grow this tomato, but I had to try.

There were others I picked just for their names too. Eva Purple Ball called to mind crushed velvet, dance cards, and the way your grandmother looked when she was very young. Mammy's sister back in Texas is named Lillian, and when I read about a tomato called Lillian's Yellow Heirloom that had been passed down from one generation of a Texas family to the next, I got homesick and had to give it a try.

My all-time favorite tomato name, though, was Radiator Charlie's Mortgage Lifter. The seed catalogs tell the story of Mr. M. C. Byles of Logan, West Virginia, who earned the nickname Radiator Charlie from the radiator repair business he opened at the foot of a steep hill on which trucks would often overheat. He didn't know the first thing about breeding plants, but after a few years of cross-pollinating the four largest tomato plants he could find, he produced a delicious—and enormous—tomato and sold the plants for a dollar each, an exorbitant price back in the 1940s. People traveled from up to two hundred miles away to buy his seedlings. Radiator Charlie raised enough money from the tomatoes to pay off the $6,000 mortgage on his house in six years.

The tomatoes in my garden were still small in early August—although a few Sungold cherry tomatoes had ripened, and some of the larger tomatoes were starting to turn colors. Though they weren't quite ripe, I had already figured out that heirloom tomatoes, even in their best moments, were funny-looking things. Brandywines are flat, misshapen fruits with deep lobes radiating out from the stem. Their skins are so thin that they would hardly survive a trip to the grocery store, which is why it is so hard to find them anywhere but at the farmers markets, where the farmers handle them as if they are made of blown glass. Many heirloom tomatoes are marked with catfacing, a kind of harmless scarring that happens when they are pollinated in cool weather, or concentric cracking, a ring of split tissue around the stem. I loved to throw these terms around once I'd learned them. Living this close to the wine country, anyone can talk about a wine's "accessibility" or its undertones of chocolate and cassis. But how many people can comment on the distinctive catfacing of Dr. Neal, or praise the perfect sugar/acid balance and light citrus notes in Amish Gold?

• • •

OVER TIME, the tomatoes became the primary focus in my garden. They had won me over, with their strange habits and peculiar names. I was determined to get them through the summer, no matter what. But I never expected that my loyalty to the tomatoes would be tested the way it was one day when I stepped outside and found a pile of finely crumbled dirt in the path next to my tomato bed, and next to it, a hole in the ground about the size of my fist. My blood froze. *Gophers.* And they had gotten to within two feet of my Brandywine.

I knew this was serious. Unlike an infestation of aphids, which can take days, weeks, or even months to kill a plant—and whose damage can often be reversed—gophers kill with swiftness and certainty. They can plow through a bed of freshly planted spring bulbs and eat every last one before they have had a chance to sprout. They can pull an entire plant into their tunnel with one swift jerk, leaving behind only a bare stake and a small hole in the ground. All my neighbors had done battle with them; I wondered why I hadn't seen any yet.

A friend of mine once told me that when she first moved to Santa Cruz, she spent the fall pouring over bulb catalogs and choosing the rarest, most exotic, and most expensive bulbs she could find for her garden. She planted hundreds of dollars' worth of bulbs, and every one was gone within ten days, thanks to the gophers. She was pretty philosoph-ical about it, shrugging her shoulders and saying to me, "Well, I bought them dinner, and I even buried it in the ground for them, so why should I be angry that they ate it?"

I had no idea how I might go about getting rid of a go-pher or a mole. I didn't think I could bring myself to kill them—after all, they are mammals, and one could even make the argument that they are *cute,* with their brown fur and little pointed noses. Mole was my favorite character in *The Wind and the Willows,* and I just can't imagine how Ratty or Mr. Toad would have felt if their little chum were poi-soned to death during a nice luncheon in the neighbor's garden, or flushed out of his snug, cozy underground home by a rush of water or poison gas.

I couldn't bring myself to trap them in a humane trap, either. I just didn't want to come face-to-face with them. There were granular poisons I could have bought and poured down their holes, but I would have felt just terri-ble about poisoning them. I would have been kept awake at night by the thought of some mother or father gopher clutching its furry brown belly in agony while the rest of the family wailed inconsolably nearby.

For a while, I thought LeRoy might be able to catch a gopher. I saw him staring down a gopher hole one after-noon, thrusting his paw in as far as it would go, his ears tilted forward to listen for any sounds from the tunnel. He looked like he was onto something. I looked around for Gray, but she was sound asleep on the kitchen floor. Her gopher-chasing days were over, but as a young cat, she had been a quick and cunning hunter. She could have given LeRoy a lesson or two if she'd felt up to it, but apparently she didn't. I stood at the back door, watching him circle the hole, his nose twitching. I took away his food dish quietly, to give an edge to his hunger.

He waited all day by that hole, and I let him. After all, he's a cat—he has no job, he can afford to spend eight hours waiting for a gopher. That afternoon, staking my tomatoes, I heard a terrified chatter and spun around: *Yes,* he had cornered one, chased it into a bushy oregano, where he took turns batting it with a paw, thrusting his head in for a better look, and pulling away in amazement when it bit his pink nose.

I sat, frozen, thinking of my fragile heirloom tomatoes, glad that my cat had at last found gainful employment. The gopher was a goner for sure. I was already beginning to wonder what I would do with the body, if LeRoy left anything behind after he killed it. Should I throw it away, or should I leave it out as an example to the other gophers?

But in a flash, the gopher darted out of the bush and LeRoy, who was accustomed to a more leisurely kill, let it skirt the flower bed and vanish, unharmed, into its hole. LeRoy was not used to dealing with animals that burrowed in the ground. He looked totally amazed that his prey had disappeared like that. He stood over the hole, bloodthirsty, whipping his tail around madly. I wanted him to learn something from this experience, to remember what could happen if he toyed with his prey too long, so I left the garden quietly, locking the door behind me, leaving him to stare forlornly down the gopher hole, wondering what had gone wrong.

CLEARLY, I COULDN'T count on LeRoy to keep the gopher population in check. I searched around in the catalogs until I found something called a Mole Chaser and decided to give it a try. This device emits an underground vibration that according to the picture on the box, sends moles and gophers scurrying out of the garden with their ears covered but otherwise unharmed. Even better, the Mole Chaser is wind powered, which meant I wouldn't have to fuss with rechargeable batteries or electrical cords. "Oh, but there's one thing," Scott said, reading the instructions while I took all the parts out of the package. "It says here you'll need a few feet of galvanized pipe."

Eight feet of galvanized pipe, to be exact. Contrary to the picture on the box, which showed gophers practically ducking to keep their heads clear of the churning wind-mill blades, this structure towered above the rest of the garden and appeared to work by sending wind-generated vibrations underground for a 100-foot radius. I put the windmill section together, ran down to the hardware store for my eight feet of half-inch galvanized water pipe, and mounted the Mole Chaser in the vegetable garden, near my half-ravaged tomato patch.

I stood watching the blades turn lazily in the afternoon breeze. The instructions reassured me that "a few minutes turning intermittently during a 24-hour period is all it takes," but I gave the blades a good fast spin anyway, then listened closely for the sound of little gopher feet running in every direction. Silence.

"How will we know if it worked?" asked Scott, skeptical but trying to be supportive all the same.

"Oh, it's working," I told him. "Just wait." I could already imagine the gophers picking up the first of these under-ground vibrations from somewhere under my vegetable garden, packing up their dishes and their books, and maybe a few family photos, and trundling off to the river for a nice long visit with Rat and Toad, who would make them feel right at home and invite them on many adventures, and even help them find a new home far away from the menacing, but otherwise harmless, vibrations of my tall, shining new Mole Chaser. It didn't get rid of the gophers altogether—they reappeared from time to time, leaving distressing holes in the ground, then disappearing again—but it lorded over the vegetable bed in a sturdy, protective way, and I never lost another tomato plant.

Tomato Trouble

In his book, *The Great Tomato Book*, Gary Ibsen remarks, "I'm sure there are many gardeners who are blessed with good soil year after year and don't need to add any fertilizer to their tomato plants." But for the rest of us, there is a full arsenal of organic tomato potions designed to strengthen the plants and protect them from pests and diseases. I use all of them, every year, and they keep the nutritional deficiencies and the wilt and the rust at bay.

Here's what I do to ensure that my tomatoes grow up big and strong:

🌱 Start seedlings in flats with a sterile seed-starting growing medium. Tomato seedlings require uniform dampness; the sterile mixture is best for preventing mold and mildew.

🐞 Provide a strong light source during germination. Tomato seedlings respond best to up to eighteen hours of sunlight as the seeds are sprouting. I haven't gotten around to buying a grow light, but I do keep my seedlings in the sunniest part of the house.

🐞 Feed early and often. I use a diluted liquid fertilizer that's high in nitrogen and designed especially for young seedlings.

🐞 Move seedlings up to four-inch pots when they are a few inches tall, and introduce them to organic potting soil at this point. Plant the seedling as deep as it will go, burying part of the stalk in soil. It will grow roots along that part of the stalk, making it stronger and more able to adapt to the outdoors.

🐞 When plants are one to two weeks from planting time (April 1 in Santa Cruz), start to harden them up, or adapt them to the outdoors, by putting them outside for a few hours a day, and gradually increase the length of time until they are spending the night outdoors as well.

🐞 Plant into ground that has been well amended with compost and manure. At planting time, feed with a balanced, organic, granular fertilizer. Add bonemeal if you've had heavy rains, to replenish the calcium that might have been washed away. This will prevent blossom end rot, the squishy gray spots that sometimes appear on the bottoms of tomatoes.

ꙮ Cover the ground with a red plastic mulch, available from some seed catalogs. The red plastic reflects light up to the plants from a particular part of the UV spectrum, encouraging bigger fruit.

ꙮ Spray periodically with copper soap, available from many organic catalogs, to prevent rust and mold.

ꙮ Spray with a mixture of dish soap and water to kill aphids. Sticky yellow traps also work well.

ꙮ Water regularly, but do not overwater. Add a granular fertilizer one more time as the plants are setting fruit.

Basil

*The herb garden should find a place on all amateurs' grounds.
Sweet-herbs may sometimes be made profitable by disposing of the
surplus to the green grocer and the druggist. The latter will often
buy all that the housewife wishes to dispose of, as the general supply
of medicinal herbs is grown by specialists, and goes into the hands
of the wholesaler and is often old when received by the local dealer.*

—L. H. BAILEY, Manual of Gardening, 1923

It always amazed me when something went
well in the garden. I usually expected the
worst: drought, disease, a plague of insects. Sometimes,
though, things just work out, in spite of everything.
That's the way it was with basil, but not at first. I planted
a row of it around my tomatoes earlier in the year,
knowing full well what I was doing: setting out five dollars' worth of herbs for the snails' breakfast the next

morning. There was only one possible fate for basil in my garden, that of getting eaten right down to the stem, until there was nothing but a slimy little nub left to the stalk, and then that would disappear, too. So far I had grown basil in clay pots on the porch, I had planted it inside a barrier of copper strips, and I had set it out among the chives and cilantro to confuse the bugs. None of these early efforts yielded me anything more than the pleasure of an afternoon in the sun spent planting deliciously fragrant young seedlings.

I had seen other people grow basil. I knew that it could be done. I visited friends who had a little knot herb garden featuring every color and variety of basil: purple opal basil, lemon basil, the enormous lettuce leaf basil, the bushy miniature Greek basil. So much basil, the owners of this garden complained, that they had grown tired of pesto every night. So much basil that they were using it to flavor vinegar and hanging the rest up to dry for the winter. Would I like some? they asked eagerly, as if they were passing their sweaters on to a poor relative. Would I do them the favor of taking some home?

I went to a farm where a row of basil stretched almost to the horizon. Basil season was nearly done; the leaves were tough and strong; the customers in the farmers markets had moved on to pungent, woody herbs like thyme and marjoram to flavor their stews and their roasted pump-kin soups. The farmer had let the basil go to seed. It acted as a magnet for bees, drawing them to his fields to buzz around the tiny white flowers and move on to pollinate his fall crops. A few more weeks and I'll rip it out, he told me, and gave the row of sweet basil an impatient look, as if to say, I've had about all of *this* I'm going to take.

I allowed these experiences to convince me that I, too, could grow basil, in the cold and the fog, right in the mid-dle of the insect battleground that is my garden. I had al-ready planted it three times within a couple of months, each time in a matter-of-fact way, quite casually, as if this were an ordinary event that would yield ordinary results. I didn't want to alarm the basil. I planted it in a row, along with everything else, and I didn't let on that I was already sick with doubt and worry, that my hopeful basil seedlings had really been more *condemned* than *planted*.

The fourth time, though, something different happened. I planted two cherry tomatoes along the retaining wall in the front of my house, where they could trail down the wall, lean over the steps coming up to the porch, and offer themselves to passersby walking down the sidewalk on their way to the beach. I took great care in digging the bed, in pulling out all the morning glory and the African daisy, hauling off some of the old clay dirt and bringing in compost from the nursery. I covered the bed with black plastic to warm the soil and keep the weeds down. I built a bamboo and twine trellis for the seedlings and planted them on the first day of May.

Something was wrong, though. The place looked bare and artificial, between the black plastic and the cement wall. It would be months before the tomatoes grew tall enough to be interesting to look at. I may as well plant something around the edge, I thought. Something that would fill in and bloom quickly and entertain until the cherry tomatoes, the guests of honor, arrived.

I went to the nursery and came home with blue annual salvia and sweet basil. I would alternate them, I decided, so that when the basil got eaten, the salvia could fill in and cover up the places where the basil would get nibbled away. The tall blue spikes of flowers would attract some bees and provide a cheerful contrast to the orange cherry tomatoes and yellow pear tomatoes that were on the way.

I checked the basil frequently after I planted it, expecting to see holes nibbled out of the larger leaves and a slimy trail leading away. Nothing. The basil was perfect, untouched. The next day was the same, and the day after that. The basil and the salvia grew at about the same rate, getting leafy and robust. The black plastic warmed the soil, the weeds stayed away, the tomatoes grew. It was as if a patch of someone else's garden had broken away and wandered over to my yard by mistake.

Then, at the height of summer, there it was: a little vegetable bed that practically dripped tomatoes, surrounded by a robust hedge of salvia and basil. The spiky blue flowers came inside and sat in a glass jar on a windowsill. The basil found its way into every meal: the tomato sandwiches, the pesto linguine, the cream cheese on bagels, even the green salads, where I snipped it into ribbons and tossed it with the lettuce. I was nonchalant about it. I didn't want the basil to think there was anything unusual going on and get worried. The snails, I had come to believe, could smell fear. So I cut and harvested and cooked and dried, until I found myself at the office one morning with two bulging plastic bags in my hand. I am overrun with basil, I heard myself saying to my office-mates. Would you like to take some home?

Too Much Basil: Pesto by Hand

There's a simple way and a complicated way to enjoy surplus basil. The simple way is this: Slather two pieces of bread with mayonnaise, top with whole basil leaves and sliced tomatoes, and eat. The complicated way? Pesto, made by hand, the old-fashioned way.

I once read an article extolling the virtues of making pesto by hand with a mortar and pestle. Yes, of course, I thought. The finer qualities of pesto can only be appreciated if it is pounded out by hand, with no electronic gadgets involved. What better way to pay tribute to my bumper crop of basil? I dusted off my marble mortar and pestle and followed the instructions carefully, but after half an hour of pounding, I had nothing more than a collection of bruised basil leaves and some misshapen chunks of garlic. Finally, I gave up and threw it all in the blender, and five minutes later, I was eating my electronically produced, second-rate pesto, and I was perfectly happy about it.

But here's the handmade pesto recipe anyway, if you want to try it. I'm told that a wide-bottomed pestle, one that nearly fills the inside of the mortar, is the key to success. Maybe I'll give it another go myself.

Pound one or two cloves of garlic with a big pinch of course salt until you've made a smooth paste. Pound in three tablespoons of pine nuts, then add two cups of shredded basil leaves, just a little at a time and pound until you can see hardly any pieces of basil leaf. Mix in about five tablespoons of shredded parmesan (you can put down your pestle and use a spoon now), then stir in about three tablespoons of olive oil, and serve. Should feed four to six very grateful people.

Surplus Produce

It is a thrill to possess shelves well stocked with home-canned food. In fact, you will find their inspection— often surreptitious—and the pleasure of serving the fruits of your labor comparable only to a clear conscience or a very becoming hat.

—IRMA S. ROMBAUER, The Joy of Cooking, 1931

Pretty soon, all the tomato plants in my garden were producing. At first we ate them raw, sliced and arranged on a plate with some of my sturdy green basil. Then we started making pasta sauce, and chilled tomato soups, and once I even tried to make my own sundried tomatoes in the oven (it didn't work). I thought I'd tried every tomato recipe ever invented. As the season wore on, I even started to get a little bored with them. Everything, it seemed, was overripe. The garden was running amuck. I couldn't keep up with it. It made me tired, just thinking about going out there and picking another tomato, and then having to bring it inside and decide what to do with it.

The squash plants were even worse. I had planted three kinds from a "summer squash sampler" of seeds I found at San Lorenzo, but somehow I got the seeds all mixed up when I planted them, and I didn't know which plant was which. I didn't think this would matter until one day I realized that what appeared to be a yellow crookneck squash had suddenly started growing as if spawned by aliens, turning a deep, hard yellow and swelling to the size of a large meatloaf. Every few days, I walked over and stood looking down at it, hoping it would have made some sort of change that would reveal to me whether I should harvest it or let it continue to grow. My friends came over for dinner one night and stood around staring at it. It was a freak of nature, springing out of an otherwise ordinary vegetable garden. It embarrassed me a little. It was enormous, excessive, ridiculous.

I WAS QUICKLY LEARNING that the biggest garden chore in August was dealing with all the extra vegetables. "August," joked a woman down the street, "the month when everybody drives with their windows up for fear someone will sneak a zucchini in." There is even a holi-day—August 8—called National Sneak Some Zucchini on Your Neighbor's Porch Night. I was ready for the holiday by the time it rolled around. I had been eating squash bur-ritos, zucchini lasagna, and fried zucchini. I didn't think I could face one more zucchini. I put my extras in a paper sack and left them on Charlie and Beverly's front porch, along with a note reminding them of the holiday.

At last, the vegetable garden had taken off, and it looked like a farm stand gone wild: bean-laden vines reach-ing toward the sky, onions bursting out of the soil, Brandy-wines and Lillian's Yellow Heirlooms turning red and gold at last. Mammy's Holland tomatoes were so plentiful that I started making sauce of out of them and freezing it. A volunteer squash—perhaps it was a pumpkin—wound its way through the sunflowers. The oregano that I bought as a seedling in a two-inch pot sprawled into a three-foot-tall mound, sporting a dazzling display of pink flowers visited constantly by bees.

"Good God," Scott said when he got home from work and wandered out into the vegetable garden. "What are you going to *do* with all this food? It's practically leaping out of the ground!"

This is exactly what a garden full of ripe produce does: It leaps out at you, begging to be picked, demanding to be watered and fed so it can produce more. My Sungold cherry tomato plant spilled over its five-foot support and practically lunged at me when I walked past it, holding out branches heavy with fruit. At first, I thought of Sungolds as a light garden snack. I would pop one or two in my mouth when I walked by, then forget about them. In August, though, they started turning ripe so quickly and in such profusion that I felt obligated to stand in the garden and eat an entire meal of cherry tomatoes, just to keep them from going to waste. I began to feel like I was in some sort of reverse *Little Shop of Horrors,* in which a wild, overgrown plant feeds me and feeds me until I beg for mercy.

I would like to think that this sudden success in the garden had something to do with my own hard work. After all, I spent so much time adding manure and compost, fertilizing, and double-digging the beds. I turned a neglected patch of solid clay into the kind of soil that gardeners dream about: a loose, friable loam that is quick-draining and full of worms. I sprinkled it with fish emulsion, I planted calendula around its edges to draw in the pollinators. Whatever the reason, all I knew was that the Curse of Late Summer had arrived. I had more food in the garden than Scott and I could eat.

Giving surplus produce away seemed like the very best way to handle the overabundance. For a while an elderly man lived nearby and left sacks of lemon cucumbers on doorsteps all up and down the street. Charlie used to stop me in the morning on the way to work. "Could you use some lemon cucumbers?" he would ask, hopefully.

I always just smiled and hoisted my lunch of lemon cucumber sandwiches and lemon cucumber salad. "Nope! I'm all set!" I would say, and drive off quickly.

But now it was my turn to give away vegetables. I left zucchini and tomatoes on porches up and down the street and brought bags of mustard and lettuce greens into the office for my coworkers to take home for dinner. I bought a vegetable dehydrator and dried peppers, onions, and beans for winter soup. Finally, I decided to try my hand at canning.

Home canning is something that no child of the suburbs grows up knowing how to do. I had no memories of a grandmother's farmhouse kitchen to draw on; my grandmothers were all too happy to stock their pantry from the supermarket. Canning for them had been a practical necessity; they saw no charm in it, and among the recipes I inherited from them when they died I found not a single mention of pickles or preserves.

Fortunately, Scott's Aunt Barbara sent a copy of her mother's famous dilly green tomato recipe. I decided to use this as a starting point for making not just green tomatoes, but also bread-and-butter pickles and tarragon-pickled green beans.

My great-grandmother Mammy had plenty of memories of canning. She approached it the way she approached everything else in her life—as a domestic art form, an ordinary experience that was magical nonetheless. She described the process to me in far greater detail than the brochure that came with the box of canning jars I bought at the hardware store. Boil the jars for a good long while, she said. It takes time to get the vegetables all picked and trimmed down to a size that will fit in the jars, so you may as well keep them sterilizing. Wrap a towel around the jars while you boil them so they won't knock into each other in the rolling water. Keep one jar out, and use it to double-check that your green beans aren't too long and that your cucumber slices aren't too fat to fit in the jar. Don't bother boiling the vegetables the way the cookbooks used to advise—the vinegar will kill the bacteria and the vegetables will stay crisper, anyway. And don't use that fancy white wine vinegar they sell these days—the acidity is never exactly right, and besides, they sell plain white Heinz vinegar in big plastic jugs for just a couple of dollars. And isn't the whole point to be economical? To save money?

She was very reassuring on the point of hygiene. "Scott's afraid I'll do this wrong and poison somebody," I told her.

It was true. He didn't want to come anywhere near my pickles.

"Oh, for heaven's sake," Mammy said. "I've put up thousands of jars of pickles and tomatoes and corn in my life, and I never lost a jar."

When I told this to Scott, he looked at me, alarmed, over the top of his glasses. "Notice she said she'd never lost a *jar,*" he said. "What about a person?"

"Oh, *right,*" I said, laughing. "What's wrong with canning, anyway? That's how people used to get through the winter, you know. On the stuff they canned and dried and kept in the cellar."

"Yeah, but who do you know who does that anymore? I swear, you must be the youngest person canning in America."

He may have been right. I didn't know anybody under the age of seventy who could give me any canning advice. But between Mammy's reassurances and Aunt Barbara's recipes, I got through it, filling each sterile jar with crisp raw vegetables, pouring in the vinegar and pickling spices, and screwing the lids on carefully, making sure I had a good seal before I put them back in their boiling water bath for one final processing. It was hot and steamy work, standing over vats of vinegar in the kitchen, but the would-be farmer in me liked the idea of preserving part of the harvest for the winter. At the end of the day, a row of pickled vegetables lined the windowsill, and the sun came through them, casting a pale green light around the room. I sat with my chin in my hand and looked at them, satisfied with my first year's harvest canned and put away for winter.

Aunt Barbara's Dilly Green Tomatoes

Okay, so canning is no picnic. The kitchen is steaming hot, and it's August to boot. Everything smells like vinegar. Your eyes water. You've used every pot in the kitchen. But there is something so worthwhile about the whole process, something so *pastoral,* about putting away the summer's bounty for the winter.

So if you want to try it, you're in luck. I have Aunt Barbara's mother's recipe for Dilly Green Tomatoes, and if you don't have any green tomatoes you want to use, try it with green beans, cucumbers, or zucchini.

> 5 cloves garlic
>
> 5 stalks celery
>
> 5 small, hot green peppers like serrano or jalepeño

1 bunch dill

1 quart vinegar

1 cup salt

10–15 small to medium green tomatoes

Yield: 5 one-quart jars

Wash green tomatoes and cut into quarters if they are too large to fit into quart jars.

Sterilize quart jars and lids by boiling in hot water for 10 minutes, then pack in green tomatoes. To each jar, add a clove of garlic, a stalk of celery, a pepper, and a piece of dill.

Combine 2 quarts water with the vinegar and salt. Bring to a boil, then fill jars to one half-inch from the top with the hot liquid.

Seal jars tightly with lids and cook in a hot-water bath, ensuring that water covers the lids of the jars by one inch, for 20 minutes. Store for at least a month before using, and refrigerate after opening.

Fall Migration

The closing scenes are not necessarily funereal.
A garden should be got ready for winter as well as for summer.
When one goes into winter quarters he wants everything neat and
trig. Expecting high winds, we bring everything into close reef.

—CHARLES DUDLEY WARNER,
My Summer in a Garden, 1870

Autumn came slowly to Santa Cruz. The trees didn't change color. No frost accumulated on the ground. In fact, autumn here looked suspiciously like summer everywhere else in the country, with clear, sunny skies and surprisingly warm afternoons. I had heard people talk about year-round gardening on the West Coast, but it didn't seem right. The garden needed a rest and so did I. The canning and freezing had all been a little overwhelming, so as the days got shorter and the tomatoes and squash stopped producing, I was almost glad to see them go. I had not planned for a fall vegetable garden; Brussels sprouts and butternut squash should have been planted in August, and I should have started some lettuce and snap pea seeds in September. But late summer drifted into fall and I didn't once think about gearing up for another gardening season. By October, when I began to miss the daily supply of garden produce, it was too late to do much about it. I put in a row of kale and chard near the back door, along with some flat Italian onions and a cold-weather parsley that I'd found. Enough for an occasional winter soup, and that was all.

The flowers kept blooming with no encouragement from me, and I was glad of that when I realized that my garden would have visitors in the fall—Monarch butterflies who migrate from Canada to Mexico each autumn in search of a warmer climate for winter. Nobody knows why, but they've taken to stopping off in a particular eucalyptus grove in Santa Cruz on their way. As many as sixty thousand butterflies share the same fifteen or twenty trees, hanging from the branches in tight clusters.

It is good that the monarchs stop here to rest, because they have quite a trip ahead of them. They emerge from their chrysalis in the late summer and begin a southern migration, following a nectar corridor down to Mexico. They feed on salvia and cosmos and pincushion flower as they stream southward, and gardeners all along the coast are glad to play host to them as they travel. Mostly they will end up in Michoacán, Mexico, where they will hang from the trees in wet gray masses until spring, unable to fly in the damp cold, remaining mostly dormant, living on the food supply they stored up during the fall. When spring arrives, the females will awaken, hungry for milkweed, and the males will awaken, hungry for love.

The female shakes herself loose from the group long enough to dry her wings in the sunlight, and the male pounces on her in midair, pulling her down to the ground to mate and carrying her back up to the trees afterward. Once the female is impregnated, she begins her search for milkweed, the only food source for her young. She travels north slowly to Canada, leaving up to five hundred eggs behind as she goes, depositing each on a scrap of milkweed with a drop of glue to hold her young in place. Sometime over the summer, exhausted from the long trip, the monarchs die just as their larvae are hatching and getting ready to repeat their parents' journey.

When my Aunt D'Anna was in town from Dallas, I took her with me to see the monarchs. D'Anna and I have always been close. We understand each other, we speak the same secret language. Even now, when I see her, she leans over and whispers to me, "You're *my* child. I loaned you to your father and he never gave you back. He has all my Aretha Franklin records, too." I knew she would love the monarchs.

When we got to the eucalyptus grove, people were standing around in dignified groups, craning their necks up at the butterflies and whispering to each other as if they were in a museum. The monarchs were mostly stuck together like wet leaves clinging to the trees, only the pale dusty undersides of their wings exposed, holding onto the branches for their lives. But as the sun came out and warmed their wings, they shook themselves loose from their huddle and hundreds of them took flight at once. The sky filled with orange butterflies soaring up to the tops of the trees, then drifting calmly down again. Each wing appeared in sharp relief against the blue sky, a perfect symmetry of black, orange, and white, thousands of them floating above us.

D'Anna and I lay right down on the observation platform, among the schoolchildren tugging on their parents' sleeves and the nature enthusiasts snapping pictures. Lying there on our backs, gazing up at a sky filled with fluttering wings, it was difficult to feel anchored to the ground. They drifted down around us, landing on the platform, on our shoes, on the camera bag, then soared up again. We felt suspended in the sky with them, as if we were flying ourselves. Speech became difficult; we were in awe.

"You know . . . " I murmured. "They only live for a year. These monarchs have never been here before. But somehow they know to come to the same place every year."

D'Anna replied in a dreamy, drugged voice. "Huh . . . how do you 'spose they know where to go?"

I thought about it. "Maybe it's the signs that say, 'Monarch Sanctuary'. Maybe they can read."

She giggled. "Maybe *they* come each year to see *us*. Maybe the butterfly parents tell their children, 'Every year, in Santa Cruz, all these humans gather in a little eucalyptus grove. Nobody knows why. But it's really a spectacular sight. You should go next year on your way to Mexico.'"

A few days later, I had dinner with some friends who live a few blocks from the eucalyptus grove. "Have you seen any monarchs at your place yet?" they asked. "After they get settled, they start flying all over town. They're all over our neighborhood." The next morning, as I walked downtown for breakfast, I saw at least a dozen fluttering along the river. They were a couple of miles away from the eucalyptus grove, and as I walked, they circled the path in front of me, giving me a good glimpse of the fine detail on their wings.

THE MONARCHS SHOWED UP in my garden as well, fluttering down like autumn leaves. They landed on the last blooming sunflower; all the others had gone to seed and were getting picked apart by the sparrows. The monarchs continued through the garden, stopping at every cosmos, opening and closing their wings slowly as if they wanted to show off the contrast between their bright orange wings and the deep fuchsia petals of the cosmos. They skimmed the pincushion flowers, drinking from each one with their long, narrow tongues and moving on. I spent as much time outside with them as I could; they wouldn't be here much longer. They took advantage of the last burst of energy my garden had to offer. Before long, the rains would start again, the monarchs would head south to Mexico, and the garden would fold in on itself, going dormant and quiet until spring.

As the butterflies flew around, I tidied up the garden, getting ready for winter. I knew how wet the ground would get once the rains started; I wouldn't be able to do much outside without sinking to my ankles in mud. I put a new layer of straw down in the vegetable paths over the first layer, which had already started to decompose. San Lorenzo had put signs up the weekend before advertising cover crop seed, which, when planted, would hold the soil in place, add some nutrients over the winter, and make good "green manure" in the spring—high-nitrogen plant material that could be tilled under and allowed to compost in place, just in time for planting the spring crops. There were several to choose from—clover, rye, fava. The idea of having young fava beans to eat in the early spring appealed to me, so I bought a bag and planted them in the new vegetable beds I'd marked out a few months back. I pulled some weeds, turned the compost pile, and tucked a blue tarp around the worm bin to shelter it from the rain.

There wasn't much more to do to put the garden to bed on that October afternoon. I didn't have much time anyway—the sun was almost down, and with November right around the corner, the days would only get shorter and colder. My first year in the garden was almost over. I was about to pack up my tools and go inside when I realized that there was one more chore I should do—rip out my tomatoes. Most of them were dead already, destroyed by wilt or fungus or aphids. A few of Mammy's Holland tomatoes hung on the vine, and the Sungolds were still going strong, continuing to bloom and produce fruit, but the tomatoes had lost their peak-of-summer sweetness. I needed to get them out of the ground and plant the rest of my fava beans in their place before the ground turned cold and soggy. I put my gardening gloves back on and turned, a little reluctantly, to the tomatoes. It seemed I'd spent the whole year getting this garden started; now, suddenly, it was coming to an end.

The tomatoes came out of the ground easily. I did not bother to unwind them from their stakes; I just grabbed a stake and a few of the thicker vines and pulled. The soil seemed to cleave in half as I pulled, separating just enough to let go of the stringy brown roots. I dropped the vines, tangled up as they were with twine and bamboo stakes, in a heap on the patio, and grabbed the next plant. Each one came out, slowly, smoothly, a few overripe tomatoes dropping to the ground as I pulled. I turned the ground a little with my spade and dropped in my fava beans. There was nothing more to do. Winter was coming, and I was ready. With a few swift tugs on my tomato vines, the vegetable garden was closed for business, and the growing season was at an end. Just in time, too: There was already a damp chill in the air, and the clouds that accumulated on the horizon were more than ordinary ocean fog. They were rain clouds.

The tomato plants, along with a few aphids that had stuck it out for the whole growing season, went into a plastic bag in the garbage instead of on the compost pile, where the aphids would surely have set up camp for the winter and attacked again next spring. Before I threw them away, I picked the few remaining ripe tomatoes. I still had a little basil growing, and plenty of garlic, so I brought one last handful of produce inside to make a plate of tomatoes as a summer farewell: sliced tomatoes, ribbons of basil, chopped garlic, and the most fragrant, spicy olive oil. I wouldn't see this dish again until July or August next year. I called Scott into the kitchen and he sat down across from me at the kitchen table. As night fell in the garden, we ate those tomatoes slowly, and savored them, because it would be a long time before we tasted them again.

Cover Crops

I found out that winter cover crops are essential on the West Coast, where the winter rains can wash good garden soil away if there's nothing to hold it in place. Now I plant a cover crop every fall, and if I leave a bed planted over the winter with cool-weather crops like leeks and beets, I give it a rest in the spring by planting gorgeous, flowering crimson clover, which attracts bees all summer, draws the first of the migratory monarchs in October, and replenishes the soil with nitrogen when I till it under just before winter.

My favorite winter crop is fava. There is something so appealing about the smooth brown seeds; they are large and comforting, and I've come to associate them with the fall. I buy about two pounds of seed, which is enough to cover five hundred square feet. I pick a chilly day in late October, after the first rain, to push the beans into the wet ground with my thumb. Within a few weeks of planting, they sprout fat green stalks, and all winter I watch them grow tall and dense, crowding out the oxalis. In the spring I turn most of them under as soon as they bloom to make compost, but I can't resist keeping a few around so I can harvest the young pods for an early spring pasta made with fava beans, kale, and shaved romano cheese.

Starting Over

*I now realize that these first years were only my novitiate,
preparing myself to build my little gray garden by the sea.*

—ANNA GILMAN HILL, Forty Years of Gardening, 1938

EACH YEAR, THE GARDEN GREW A LITTLE BIGGER. I filled
the patio with red geraniums, and morning glories spilled
over the fence. The small front room became a greenhouse where I started seeds each winter for the spring
vegetable garden. I grew so many varieties of tomatoes
that I had to plant some in enormous black plastic nursery pots and put the rest out front, near the sidewalk,
where the tourists commented on them but never ripped
them out.

A shady stretch of earth along the garage wall became
a memorial garden. Gray's kidneys failed her one spring,
when she was twenty and I was twenty-seven. No one I
knew had lived with a pet as long as I had lived with Gray.
It made sense to bury her in the backyard, where I could
plant soft gray lamb's ears and forget-me-nots at her

grave. Her presence changed the garden, bringing a measure of sorrow that I'd never felt out there before. The small, dappled flower bed where she was buried eventually filled with columbine and cottage pinks, Shasta daisies and calla lilies. In the spring, the camellia and wisteria would drop their flower petals all at once, carpeting her grave in carmine red and lilac. It looked like a subdued Mardi Gras. Gray would've liked it, I think.

After a few years, Scott and I began to realize we couldn't live in Santa Cruz forever. The realization crept up on us slowly, and we were reluctant to pay it much attention at first. We loved living in a beach town: We loved the ocean, and the roller coaster, and the fact that all around us, people were on vacation. Now that Gray was buried in the garden, my heart seemed more firmly rooted in our patch of Santa Cruz soil than ever before. But while we lived there, rents had gone sky-high, and we were spending more time than ever at our office jobs just to keep up. It began to seem downright uncivilized to spend fifty or even forty hours a week in a cubicle. I had friends who had found ways to work part-time, travel, and slow down enough to enjoy their lives. I envied them. I wanted to quit my desk job and write a garden column or work in a nursery, but I couldn't afford to. It took a couple of real, full-time jobs to cover the bills in a high-priced town like Santa Cruz. I also wanted to buy a house—I wanted to own the land I gardened, not just rent it, but that, too, was out of the question. The most modest houses were selling for close to half a million dollars.

I wasn't the only one who felt that way; Scott had a long and difficult commute into Silicon Valley every day, and as he sat in his car, in the traffic and the smog, he thought about his book business, the orders waiting to be filled, the rare books waiting to be hunted down in dusty old bookstores. There is no good time to quit a day job and pursue a business of one's own. There is never enough money and there are always risks. But Scott had a lot of time to think about it during those hourlong drives over the hill and back. Life is short, he reasoned. If he didn't give it a try, he'd always wonder what he'd missed. He, too, was starting to think that the high cost of living in Santa Cruz was keeping him from doing what he really wanted to do.

Gradually, the realization came to us that we should leave Santa Cruz.

First we had to choose a place to live. We had quite a list of requirements: We wanted to stay in California, where I could garden year-round, we wanted to live within walking distance of the ocean, and we wanted to find a small town, one with lots of charming old houses to choose from. Eventually, we decided that our best choice was Eureka, where Scott used to live. It's a quaint but squarely unpretentious town filled with Victorian homes, known for its fishing harbor and its old-fashioned, brick-lined town square. The weather is very Pacific Northwest—cold, foggy, and rainy —but we decided we wouldn't mind that. Scott had had a melanoma removed a few years earlier and he was on strict orders to stay out of the sun. When people warned us about Eureka's gray, overcast weather, he smiled faintly and said, "I think I've had enough sun to last a lifetime."

We didn't act on our decision right away. We called a couple of real estate agents; we sent away for the newspaper real estate listings. The decision needed time to sink in. We looked at the ocean, we walked past the roller coaster, already shut down for winter. Neither one of us said it, but we were both thinking: Can we really give up all this?

I FOUND MYSELF WALKING through the garden a lot in those days, wondering what plants I would take with me and what I would leave behind. I had a friend who moved her garden once. She and her husband got divorced and he kept the house. They had lived in the house for eight years, and she had amassed an extraordinary collection of rare ornamental plants: tiny, fragile, wispy things smuggled from Australia that she would cover in glass cloches each winter; tropical vines; and ornamental grasses in every shade from chartreuse to spruce blue to red to black. I went over to her house one day while she was digging up her plants. She hadn't even found a new place to live yet.

"That son of a bitch," she muttered and she dug. "He told me I had to replace every plant I took." She straightened up to look me in the eye. "I planted this garden from nothing!" she said. "Marigolds! That's what he's getting. Marigolds, pansies, and goddamn *impatiens*," she said scornfully, as she looked at the broken up garden around their home.

My plants were all so ordinary—daisies, penstemon, foxglove, salvia—that for a while I didn't even think about trying to bring them with me. I could buy those plants in Eureka, I told myself, or grow them from seeds when we got there. But I wanted to take something with me from Santa Cruz, so I started digging them up, the daisies, the foxglove, anything I could safely pull out of the ground and stick in a one-gallon pot. I considered taking cuttings from the salvia and propagating them. And I even collected some seeds: pincushion flower, poppy, cosmos, and yarrow, as much as I could shake into an envelope.

There wasn't much I could take from the vegetable garden. Most of the vegetables were annuals that I started from seed every year, anyway. I considered digging up the artichokes and a few herbs. I knew I'd take Scott's oregano, the one he brought from Eureka for me to plant when we moved in here. And the asparagus was nonnegotiable—I couldn't leave it behind. We had brought it as three year-old stock, then nurtured it along in our garden, adding more roots every year. Asparagus takes patience and years of waiting before it will produce a decent-sized crop. Before we moved, I decided, I would dig up the roots and store them in a bucket of dirt for the trip to their new home, giving them a prime spot in the moving van, right next to the worm bin, whose inhabitants would be taking a longer journey than they could ever imagine, all without ever leaving the safe confines of their black plastic home.

WE SET OFF on a house-hunting trip one weekend around Thanksgiving, showing up in Eureka with a list of what we wanted in a house. We made the list on the seven-hour drive from Santa Cruz to Eureka, filling out a long questionnaire that we'd found in the back of a book about how to buy a house. Scott drove, and I read each question aloud and wrote down the answers.

"Style of architecture," I read. That one was easy: Craftsman or Victorian. Something with history, with character. No suburban ranch homes for us.

"Lot size." Another easy one. Enormous. Big as we could afford. No large shade trees, because my garden would need all the sun it could get.

"Location." Walking distance to downtown and the harbor. One thing we were giving up by moving to Eureka was easy access to the beach. The town is situated inside a sheltered harbor, and to get to a real beach, a beach with sand dunes and waves and shorebirds, we would have to get in the car and drive a few miles. So at the very least, we wanted to be able to walk after dinner, to a movie, and to the edge of the harbor, where the fishing boats unloaded every morning.

By the time we got to town, we had our list. We needed extra bedrooms for guests, for Scott's office and library, and for my study. We needed a great big kitchen. We needed a fireplace. For two people who had always lived happily in a studio apartment or a small house, we suddenly needed a lot of space.

The realtor met us at noon and took us to a few houses she'd picked out for us. Some had yards that would be too small for my garden. Others seemed cramped and dark, the wrong kind of house in a town that is dark and foggy anyway. One was right next door to a high school, and teenagers sprawled on the lawn in the afternoons. Scott and I looked at each other and thought the same thing— Teenagers. Worse than tourists. "Oh yeah," we said to the realtor, "we forgot to mention two things. No busy streets. No high schools." We went on to the next house, a perfectly restored Craftsman with a bright, airy loft and Arts and Crafts–replica fixtures throughout, but a pair of rotweillers barked at us from across the street, and a car rusted in the lawn next door. The neighborhood made us a little nervous.

Then our realtor said, "This house was just listed this morning. It's a little out of your price range, but let's go take a look," and when she pulled up in front of the freshly painted, three-story Victorian, I could hardly get a breath. It was a storybook of a house, painted a creamy white with pale orange, burgundy, and cornflower blue trim. There were two front doors, side by side, a leftover, the realtor told us, from the days when the house had been divided into two flats. Lace curtains billowed in the windows. Rhododendrons and camellias bloomed in front.

Scott and I followed the realtor inside. We walked slowly through two front parlors, a formal dining room, and a large, sunny kitchen. Upstairs there were four bed-rooms and a large bathroom with an old claw-foot tub— the bathtub I've always wanted, the bathtub I could already picture myself soaking in after a long day in the garden. Up another flight of stairs: a full attic, in need of nothing more than a little insulation and some drywall to make it into the perfect winter's retreat, with a bird's-eye view of the garden.

And what a garden it would be! Outside, there was a lot more land than we had in Santa Cruz: a long, narrow strip of front yard about fifty-five feet across and fifteen feet deep, a shady side yard next to the kitchen, and a wide, sunny yard on the other side. In back, a good forty by forty feet of open land, enough space for a vegetable garden twice as large as my garden in Santa Cruz.

We saw a few other houses that day, taking pictures and jotting down notes at each one. We got the pictures developed and took them with us to dinner that night, paging through our notes and talking over each house we saw. Scott liked another Victorian, smaller but beautifully restored, that was on a smaller parcel of land. The price was great—around $95,000—but the neighborhood seemed a little iffy and downtown was a bit too far away for a comfortable walk. Although our beautiful four-bedroom Victorian—I had already begun to call it *ours*—was priced at $129,000, the difference seemed small given all its advantages; it was so much larger, just eight or ten blocks from downtown, and in a much better neighborhood. Twenty years from now, I argued, that difference in price would seem like nothing. But the difference between the two houses would seem like everything.

Neither one of us slept that night. I dreamt about debt all night long. In my half-sleeping, half-waking state, I tried to calculate the mortgage payment, the property taxes, the insurance. I worried about whether we could rent it out during the time it would take us to get ready to move. I added up what we put into savings and retirement each month, wondering if we could scrape together the full payment if we had to. At some point during the night, Scott got up, thinking I was asleep, and went into the bathroom so he could turn on a light, page through the real estate magazines, and worry over it.

The next morning, with maybe four hours of sleep between us, we told the realtor we wanted to see the house again. We spent most of the morning looking it over. I took pictures of every room, Scott mapped out the house on a piece of paper, and we both tried to look for faults, sags, soft spots—anything that might change our minds before we made an offer. By the end of the day, we were sure of our decision. We went back to our realtor's office to write up an offer, and somehow, miraculously, by five o'clock we were on our way out of town, and our realtor was driving to the seller's agent to deliver the offer. Six weeks later, we were homeowners. The people we bought the house from hadn't found a new place yet, so we rented the house back to them and started getting ready to move.

Being a homeowner changed the way I thought about the holidays, which, by this time, were only a few weeks away. In all the years we'd been together, Scott and I had never bought a Christmas tree. Either we couldn't afford to go out and buy the tree, the stand, lights, and ornaments all at once, or we weren't going to be home during the holidays, anyway, and it seemed like a waste. Our house always felt a little barren around Christmas as a result. But now that we owned a house, I wanted us to start having our own holiday traditions, as a couple, instead of relying on our families to supply that for us during the few days we spent with them each Christmas.

I knew that somewhere, maybe in the attic, we had a box of Christmas decorations. My aunt and uncle had sent a set of tin vegetable ornaments from Texas the year before, and Scott had brought a few ornaments home from an office Christmas party. I had strings of lights that I'd bought on sale after the holidays, and an assortment of stray bows, ribbons, and garlands that I'd saved from packages. We'd gone to Santa Fe on vacation and bought dried chile peppers and a gaudy tin star tree topper.

All those decorations sat in a box marked "Xmas," waiting to be opened, while I mulled over what kind of tree I wanted. I didn't bother consulting Scott about any of it. I knew that if I picked the right tree and just brought it home, I could get him in the spirit. I was still undecided when I pulled into San Lorenzo on my lunch hour one afternoon. The jumbo six-packs of annual flowers were all gone, and in their place, an assortment of Christmas trees, wreaths, and garlands. I was worried about how LeRoy would behave around a full-sized Chrismas tree. He would probably climb right to the top, and, if the tree could support his weight, he'd hang on with one paw and push ornaments off with another. I considered buying twenty or so feet of garland and just decorating a room or a couple of windows with it. Or maybe even just a wreath . . . then I found a display of two-foot-tall living dwarf pines, lined up in rows like a tiny Christmas tree farm. This tree grows very well in containers, the sign told me, and will stay small and perfectly cone shaped, year after year.

I chose the tallest dwarf Christmas tree I could find, one that towered a good four inches above the rest, along with a redwood planter and a few feet of pine and cedar garland to lay around its base. I took it home and it sat there for a few days until I had time to decorate it.

When I pulled out the box of decorations and started untangling the lights, Scott was sitting at the computer, as usual, doing some accounting for his book business. I didn't say anything to him, but in a few minutes I heard

Elvis's "Blue Christmas" from the CD player and felt Scott standing beside me, pulling me toward the mistletoe I had just hung in the doorway. "This was a *good* idea," he whispered, smiling at our little tree and the handful of decorations. "Maybe next year we'll have Christmas in our very own house. What do you think?"

What do I think? It made a shiver run up the back of my neck, just thinking about it.

While Elvis crooned in the background, Scott untangled our string of lights and wrapped them around the tree, and we took turns hanging our seven or eight ornaments. When we were finished, I wired the star to the top of the tree. It was a little heavy for such a tiny tree, but it held up.

At night, with the lights plugged in, our tree was the finest first tree anyone ever had. It looked like the kind of tree we would have bought when we were first dating, back in our starving graduate-student days. We could have bought a huge tree, with all the trimmings, but it just seemed right to start out with this tiny creature, to bring it with us when we went to our new home, and to water it and watch it grow over the years.

Letter to the Next Gardener at 118 Buena Vista

Dear Gardener,

I feel a little silly leaving this letter behind, but I can't help but wonder who will be the next caretaker of my garden, now that I am leaving. I suppose most gardeners would want to leave a parting message behind if they could, one tentative link with the next caretaker of the garden, before leaving it for good. I feel like a mother leaving instructions to the baby-sitter, except that I am not coming back at the end of the evening. It's yours now, to do with what you wish. Still, there may be some mysteries I can solve, some secrets I can pass on.

I am a little overwhelmed at the task of moving, because I know that after all these years, I can't leave the garden behind entirely; there are parts of it that I will want to bring with me. There are seeds to collect, cuttings to propagate, bulbs to divide. After all, I have made an investment. I have spent countless hours and an unthinkable sum of money bringing this garden to life, and it would be foolish to simply abandon it. I want to carry some of the plants I brought here to my next garden, and I also want to find a way to carry some of what was already here with me when I go: the old gnarled wisteria, the reliable camellia, the early blooming crocosmia. If a cutting can be made, I will make it and bring a little seedling along with me, tucked between a lamp and a toolbox in the backseat. Like a chain letter, I will take a plant from this garden to the next, and from the next garden to the one after that, and so on, until someday I am an old woman nurturing along a patchwork quilt of a garden, with cuttings and scraps from every garden I tended before.

There are some things that I should tell you about the garden now, while they are fresh in my mind, before I am so immersed in the process of moving that I have no time to sit down and gather my thoughts. Perhaps you are coming to this garden after it has been left alone for a few years. Maybe it has even been neglected for a decade or more, while the tenants of the house kept themselves busy with less domestic pursuits. If it looks wild and overgrown, good. It was never wild enough when it was mine. I'm glad it did its work better without me, and somehow I'm not surprised.

If you come here in the winter, save your strength and let the oxalis have the run of the place. If you try to pull it up, you will strip every young bulb off the taproot, leaving a dozen offspring in the ground for next year. Yes, it will take over the entire garden for a few months. Yes, it will crowd out the young seedlings and the tender bulbs. I tried for years to eradicate the oxalis, but it couldn't be done. Think of it as an exercise in letting go, in a sort of Zen-like permissiveness that you might never allow yourself the rest of the year.

I'm sorry about the lemon tree. I lavished all my love on the orange tree, fertilizing it, picking it clean of bugs, pruning judiciously. I started with thick-skinned, bitter fruit and ended with sweet, juicy Valencias. I staved off colds every winter with the fruit from that tree. Meanwhile, the lemon tree suffered. I made a few drastic cuts to remove some old, half-dead branches, but it never produced more than a few edible lemons a year. Looking at it now, I notice that the leaves are yellow. It probably has an iron deficiency. It was careless of me to ignore it, and I have no excuse. But do try to nurse it along if you can.

Don't give up on the fuchsia or the wisteria. They are old plants, and their branches are surprisingly light and brittle, like the bones of old women. But if you feed them and prune them just a little now and then, they will reward you with a modest show of flowers every spring.

Oh—and if a volunteer tomato emerges over the summer, encourage it. More likely than not, you have been blessed with Sungold, the sweetest cherry tomato I ever tasted. I grew Sungolds every year that I lived here, and by the end of the season the tomato bed was littered with the excess fruit. It will spring out of one former tomato bed or another if you let it, and if you're not a cherry tomato lover already, it will win you over.

If there are any roses along the side yard, it is only because I failed to eradicate them entirely. They are horrid, sickly things, good for nothing, incapable of more than a few token blooms. Dig them out, if you can, or whack them down to the ground, but don't fall prey to their pretty rose garden promises. They will only disappoint you.

Yes, I am responsible for the forget-me-nots. I planted one simple row of them and now they are everywhere: in the vegetable beds, among the ground covers, even sprouting in the planters on the front porch, all the result of an unfortunate combination of sticky little burrlike seeds and an adventurous young cat who loved to romp through the garden. Well, there are worse weeds than forget-me-nots, and at least you will have something to pick in February and to keep in very small jars on the windowsill.

I do have one request, if you'll pardon me for making demands on a garden that after all I chose to leave. But I feel some responsibility to ask this: If you can, please leave the spot between the wisteria and the camellia, under the eaves of the shed, untouched. If nothing has changed, you'll know the spot because it is covered with lamb's ears. I know it will be tempting, particularly since you'll probably have the sense to knock down that old shed and either expand the garden, or pave over more of it to make room for a modern, double-car garage. But I had to leave a pet behind in that spot, and I just can't bear the thought of her getting tilled up or paved over. Leave her there, if you can—it is a peaceful, quiet spot, and I'm sure you'll be glad you kept it just as it is.

Maybe it's a little crazy for me to write a letter like this. After all, we don't really own the land, do we? We just occupy it. Gardening taught me this. I moved onto this piece of land and knew immediately that someone had been there before me. The daffodil bulbs scattered along the fence, the ancient florabunda, the citrus trees, all pointed to a long-ago gardener with ambitious plans. But these plants didn't tell the whole story. They were newcomers, too. Once, digging in the garden, I found a piece of stone, chipped into a crude blade. Someone was here long before me, crouched on a bare bluff overlooking the river, before the settlers arrived and colonized the rim of land around the bay. This piece of earth was never mine, and not just because I rented rather than owned it. Land is the one thing that can't be moved, that I can't bring with me. It will remain here for the next generation, and the generation after that, and it will tolerate our pounding on it and digging into it the best it can.

I hope that I have left the garden in better condition than when I arrived. It may be weedy and unkempt when you find it, but just wait. I'm sure the cosmos will self-sow, and the yarrow will hold its own against the oxalis, and somewhere, in the wilderness, in the gentle tangle, the butterflies and the bees will return, as they have for years. Wishing you luck and patience and plenty of sun—

Amy Stewart

Acknowledgments

I WOULD LIKE TO THANK my parents for their fine examples of hard work and dedication to their art, and my brother Jason for setting the bar for artistic accomplishment in our family very, very high. Thanks to David and Nikki Sands, Annette Brooks, and Chris Fore for their warm and loving support. Four great writers, Carl Klaus, Carolyn Flynn, Wendy Counsil, and Beverly Levine, read the manuscript and provided their valuable comments early on. Thanks to Trayce Lea Lawson, editor of *La Gazette,* and Pat Stone, editor of *GreenPrints,* who have published certain sections of this book in revised form over the years. My agent Blanche Schlessinger believed in this book from the beginning, and my editor at Algonquin, Antonia Fusco, saw it through to completion with confidence, skill, and patience.

I owe a great debt to Bookshop Santa Cruz and Capitola Book Café. I did research in these two bookstores, wrote entire chapters there, and sometimes just showed up after a difficult day's work to drop into an armchair and breathe the intoxicating scent of completed books. I couldn't survive as a writer without a bookstore nearby.

Finally, I extend all my gratitude to my husband, Scott Brown, for his extraordinary patience and kindness, his good humor, and his generous faith in this book and in me.